Inside
Intuition

inside
intuition

What We Know About Nonverbal Communication

FLORA DAVIS

McGRAW-HILL BOOK COMPANY

New York   St. Louis   San Francisco   Düsseldorf   London
Mexico   Sydney   Toronto

Library of Congress Cataloging in Publication Data

Davis, Flora.
    Inside intuition.

    1. Nonverbal communication.   I. Title.
BF637.C45D35   153   72-8070
ISBN 0-07-015563-1

To Rebecca and Jeffrey

Preface

I am the kind of person who doesn't quite trust telephones. Not because I believe the telephone system is falling apart—though it often seems that it is—but because over the phone I have no way to be sure what the other person really means. If I can't see him, how can I guess what he's feeling? And what does it matter what he says, a lot of the time, if I don't know that?

Perhaps it was because of this bias of mine that I was so intrigued when one day, well over four years ago, I picked up *The New York Times* and found in it a news story about a new field of research—nonverbal communication. Subsequently, I was assigned to write an article on it for *Glamour* magazine. But when I finished my research three or four months later, I had the feeling that I'd barely scratched the surface, that there was much, much more to learn.

I rarely do an article without being tempted to try out a new career. When I interview an anthropologist, I wind up wishing I could become one. If I spend an hour consulting a psychotherapist, I emerge into the gritty New York sunlight wondering why on earth I wanted to be a writer when I could conceivably have stuck with psychology in college and ended up a therapist. It's never so much the job that intrigues me as the subject itself.

Anyway, after several months' exposure to nonverbal communication, the effect was even more profound than usual: I was hooked and I couldn't bear to let go. So I spent the next year and a half traveling to universities and mental institutions, because that's where much of the research on communication is being done. I interviewed anthropologists, psychologists, psychiatrists: a fair sampling of the people involved in the field. I looked at reels and reels of film, bland black-and-white films of people sitting around and talking, or standing around and talking. Usually, the film was run through for me in slow motion, so that the voices and the body movements themselves had an eerie, dreamlike, underwater quality. Gradually, from looking at films, I began to see. Not as much as the scientists see—one of them told me it would take two years to actually train me—but better than I had ever been able to see before.

Because to see is what it's all about, I suggest that the reader start this book by sitting down in front of a television set. Switch it on, leaving the picture on and the sound turned off. I recommend talk shows—Dick Cavett and Johnny Carson in particular—for this, because the people are behaving, not acting, and the camera pulls back from time to time to give you full-length body views. With the usual verbal distractions removed, your first impression will probably be of the sheer, confusing quantity of body motion. At any given instant, too many things seem to be happening too fast. A man raises his eyebrows, cocks his head, uncrosses his legs, leans back in his chair, forms a steeple with his fingers; and then seconds later his hands begin to beat the air in emphatic gestures as he begins to speak.

If you were a scientist confronted with these images, what would you study? How would you record what you saw? Where would you begin?

Just in the past few years, hundreds of social scientists have made these choices and have begun concentrated efforts to crack the nonverbal code. It's their efforts, their discoveries, that this book is about.

Let me say right at the start, however, that this is no code book. It offers no simple ways to psych out another person's secrets through his nonverbal behavior. Nor will you be able to sit down in front of that speechless TV set and translate body motions as if there were an easily understood vocabulary of the body: as if a hand steeple invariably meant just one thing and a left-to-right leg cross another. Human communication is much too complex for that, and in any case communication research is still a fledgling science.

I do think the day may come when you will be able to take courses in decoding nonverbal behavior, and I'm not at all sure that will be a good thing, especially if they promise too much.

Nevertheless, we all have the ability to decode to some degree. We call it intuition. We learn it in babyhood and use it all our lives on a subconscious level, and that's much the most efficient way to do it. In a flash, we interpret a body movement or react to a tone of voice, and we read it in as part of the whole message, which is clearly better than consciously juggling several dozen different message components, some of which may actually contradict one another.

What I hope this book will do for readers is what writing it has done for me: it has added a number of curious pleasures to my life. I now trust my own intuition, sometimes to the point of foolhardiness. And I can often tell where it comes from. When I have an impression that someone is secretly angry, for example, I know some of the things he has done with his body that gave me that impression. I still go by an overall feeling for the situation and not by any intellectual analysis, but for my own satisfaction, and much to my delight, I can often partially explain that feeling.

Another thing I've found is that television and films hold a new interest for me, especially when I happen to see something through a second time. I can sit back and enjoy the subtle nuances of a good actor's performance, can analyze the effect it has when he leans back in his chair at one point and then leans forward abruptly at another.

At parties, or when I'm with a small group, I find that my attention occasionally snags on something nonverbal. I once registered, for example, the fact that two men sitting at opposite ends of a sofa had put their feet up on it—legs bent, knees splayed—in identical and unusual postures. In a silent fellowship of the body, they were as alike as a pair of bookends, except that one of them, the one who had come to ask for advice, had his arm stretched out along the back of the sofa, opening himself toward his friend, while the other leaned back with arms folded noncommittally, clearly expressing—or so it seemed to me—some basic reservations.

On another occasion, when a friend said to me at the end of an evening, "I felt you were somehow withdrawn tonight, that we really weren't very together," it wasn't easy to leap in with hasty denials when I could think back and recall in body-motion terms some of what I had done to give him that impression. There have been times when I haven't been exactly grateful for what I've learned about nonverbal behavior. It's hard enough to take responsibility for all the things that can slip out verbally in conversation, without feeling that you need to explain a particular posture, to justify where you stood, where you looked or failed to look, and the particular arrangement of your arms and legs.

Self-consciousness is a problem for many people when they first become aware of the fact that body motion communicates. It attacked me so acutely at times that I was momentarily half-paralyzed. Interviewing the scientists was particularly intimidating. By the time I'd listened to three of them talk about palm-presentation—an open-handed gesture often made by Anglo-Saxon women when they are attracted to a man—I was practically sitting on my hands. But eventually I came to accept what one of the experts suggested to me: that people can be as alike or as different as the leaves on a tree and that the scientists seldom take note of a gesture unless it's something really unusual.

In a way, it was liberating to realize just how out-in-front my own emotions had always been; to realize that all along people had understood intuitively much more than I told them in words about how I felt, what I really meant, how I was reacting; and that they had accepted it and presumably still would, even the communication experts for whom body messages sometimes come through not in code but in clear.

And once I got beyond self-consciousness, I found I'd gained a very special kind of awareness: a new sensitivity to what others were feeling and even an occasional surprising insight into my own reactions.

And I'd learned beyond a doubt that the part of the message that's visible is at least as important as the part that's audible. Eventually I learned, too, that nonverbal communication is more than just a system of emotional cues and that it can't, in fact, really be separated from verbal communication. The two are woven together inextricably, for when human beings meet face to face, they communicate simultaneously on many levels, conscious and subconscious, and use most of their senses—sight, sound, touch, smell—to do it. And then they integrate all that by using the decoding device that's sometimes called the sixth sense: intuition.

Acknowledgements

In writing this book, I have had the help of a great number of people. It was Professor Erving Goffman, for example, who started me on the long road to publication when, in the course of an interview, he provided me with a tantalizing overview of the subject. Professor Ray L. Birdwhistell was especially generous with his time and suggestions, as were Dr. Adam Kendon, Dr. Albert Scheflen, Dr. Paul Ekman, Ms. Martha Davis, Mrs. Irmgard Bartenieff, Professor William Condon, Dr. Eliot Chapple, and Dr. Paul Byers.

Others were also enormously helpful; they answered questions, sent me material, and told me where I could find more. And so in addition I would like to express my gratitude to Dr. Christopher Brannigan, Professor Edward Cervenka, Professor Starkey Duncan, Jr., Professor Ralph Exline, Professor Edward T. Hall, Professor Eckhard H. Hess, Professor Carroll E. Izard, Professor Sidney Jourard, Dr. Augustus F. Kinzel, Dr. Robert E. Kleck, Professor George F. Mahl, Dr. Melvin Schnapper, Professor Thomas A. Sebeok, Professor Robert Sommer, Professor Silvan Tomkins, Professor Henry Truby, Dr. Ian Vine, and Dr. Harry Wiener.

Dr. Mamu Tayyabkhan and Ms. Karen Davis patiently read the manuscript for me and were my toughest critics and warmest supporters. Ms. Joan Fredericks also, at one crucial point, gave me the benefit of her editorial experience and advice.

Last, my special thanks to Rebecca and Jeffrey Davis, who from time to time cheerfully agreed to "baby-sit" each other, so that I could get just a little more work done.

Contents

xvi *Contents*

The Fledgling Science 1

The concept of nonverbal communication has fascinated nonscientists for centuries. Sculptors and painters have always been aware of how much can be conveyed in a gesture or by a posture, and nonverbal skills are the actor's stock in trade. The novelist who relates that a character "stubbed out his cigarette viciously" or "rubbed his nose thoughtfully" dips into a shared folklore of gesture. Psychiatrists, too, have always been acute observers, noting the nonverbal idiosyncracies of their patients, and making a practice of pointing them out and interpreting them.

But not until early in this century did any real research on nonverbal communication begin. From about 1914 to 1940, there was considerable interest in how people communicate by their facial expressions. Psychologists ran dozens of experiments—but the results were disappointing, so much so that the experimenters came to the rather remarkable conclusion that the face does not express emotions in a reliably recognizable way.

During that same period, anthropologists pointed out that body motions are not random, but learned like a language. Edward Sapir wrote, "We respond to gestures with an extreme alertness and, one might almost say, in accordance with an elaborate code that is written nowhere, known by none, and understood by all." But, for the most part, the anthropologists made no real attempt to decipher the code, and it wasn't until the nineteen fifties that a handful of men—among them Ray L. Birdwhistell, Albert E. Scheflen, Edward T. Hall, Erving Goffman, and Paul Ekman—finally tackled it in a systematic way.

For a long time even after that, communication research was an esoteric specialty. The researchers involved were individualists, often working separately and alone, and mavericks, since they committed themselves to a field that was at the time barely respectable scientifically. As one of them put it, "There was a time when we all knew each other; we were like a clique. And when we went out to lecture to professional groups what we got back, very often, was a kind of rejecting curiosity."

All that has changed. The new scientific enthusiasm for communication research has its roots in the groundwork done by the pioneers in the field, but the enormous public interest in nonverbal communication seems to be part of the spirit of the times, the need that many people feel to get back in touch with their own emotions—the search for the emotional truth that perhaps gets expressed nonverbally.

Communication research is the offspring of five different disciplines: psychology, psychiatry, anthropology, sociology, and ethology. It is a young and contentious science, with findings and research tactics often hotly disputed. Even a sketchy consideration of the different viewpoints and methodologies involved explains the disputes. The psychologist, for example, in looking at the whole stream of body motion, has in general picked out units of behavior to study: perhaps eye contact, smiling, touching, or some combination of these, and he has studied them in a fairly traditional way. While his experiment is in progress, dozens of college students pass through his laboratory. Usually, they are given a task to distract their attention and then their nonverbal behavior is recorded on film, to be analyzed later and processed into statistics.

On the other hand, the experts in kinesics (pronounced kĭ-nē′-siks and meaning the study of body motion) generally favor the systems approach. Kinesicists come from a variety of scientific backgrounds. This new field of research has an anthropologist for a founding father and has attracted psychiatrists, psychologists and others. One of its basic tenets is the belief that communication cannot be studied a unit at a time. It is an integrated system and must be analyzed as a whole, with attention paid to how every element relates to every other element. The kinesicists often take their cameras out into the field—to zoos, parks, city streets—and some maintain that psychologists who do their filming in a laboratory run the risk of catching only strained and artificial behavior. Analyzing their own films run in slow motion, the kinesicists have discovered a level of communication where people signal and respond so swiftly and subtly that the message, though it obviously has impact, never quite reaches awareness.

Psychiatrists have long recognized that the way an individual moves his body provides clues to his character, his emotions, and his reactions to the people around him. Over a period of many years, Felix Deutsch recorded the couch-postures and gestures of his patients. Other psychiatrists have done film analysis and still others have agreed to be filmed or observed while treating patients. More and more therapists are using films and videotapes to study behavior and as tools in the process of treatment. Patients confronted with video images of themselves are encouraged to react to the way they look and move, and to learn from their own behavior, verbal and nonverbal, in a group.

Then there are the sociologists, who have observed and described a kind of subliminal etiquette to which nearly all of us conform and which shapes our behavior in both large and small ways. For example, we all know how to avoid a head-on collision on a busy sidewalk, though we would be hard put to say exactly how we do it. We know how to react when an acquaintance picks his nose in public; and how to appear involved but not overinvolved in a conversation.

Anthropologists have looked at the different cultural idioms in the language of the body and have discovered that an Arab and an Englishman, a black American and a white one, really do not move in quite the same ways.

Ethologists have made their contribution, too. In several decades of studying animals in the wild, they have turned up startling similarities between the nonverbal behavior of man and that of the other primates. Struck by this phenomenon, some are now turning to "human ethology," studying how people court, raise their young, dominate others or signal submission, quarrel and make up. This very concrete physical behavior can then be compared with the way monkeys and apes handle the same relationships.

Lastly, there are the experts in Effort-Shape, a system for recording body motion that is derived from dance notation. What they are attempting to develop is a way to deduce facts about a man's character not from the particular movements he makes but from his whole style of movement.

George du Maurier once wronte, "Language is a poor thing. You fill your lungs with wind and shake a little slit in your throat, and make mouths, and that shakes the air; and the air shakes a pair of little drums in my head . . . and my brain seizes your meaning in the rough. What a roundabout way and what a waste of time."

And so it might be, if words were all. But they are only the beginning, for beyond words lies the bedrock on which human relationships are built—nonverbal communication. Words are beautiful, exciting, important, but we have overestimated them badly—since they are not all or even half the message. In fact, as one scientist suggested, "Words may be what men use when all else fails."

2 | Gender Signals

When a baby is born, the first thing everyone wants to know is its sex. In the early days of life the difference may seem mostly anatomical, but as the infant grows older, it begins to behave like a boy or like a girl. To what extent this behavior is due to basic biology and to what extent it is learned is, of course, a controversial question. Some feminists insist that all the behavioral differences are learned and that, leaving aside the obvious physiological discrepancies, women are the same as men. Other people say that men are men and women are women, and that for biological reasons the two sexes look, behave, and even move quite differently. Kinesics has turned up a certain amount of evidence to back the feminists.

It seems that from the time a baby is born we tell it hundreds of times a day in subtle, nonverbal ways whether it is a boy or a girl. Most people actually hold a girl baby differently than they do a boy—in our society, boys, even at a very early age, are apt to be handled more roughly.

Every time a boy baby acts in a way that accords with our convictions about how a boy ought to act, we reinforce his behavior. The reinforcement can be something as subtle as an approving tone of voice or a fleeting, approving facial expression, or it can be quite verbal and specific (indulgently: "Isn't that just like a boy?"). And of course we reward a girl for showing feminine traits. Little boys may not be scolded for wanting to play with dolls, but they are seldom encouraged to. Perhaps the total absence of any response—the lack of positive vibrations—tells the boy he is doing something boys are not meant to do.

It is certain that on some subliminal level we also reward or fail to reward far subtler behavior, for at some point in their development boys begin to move and hold their bodies like males and girls to move like females. These ways of moving are learned rather than innate— they vary from culture to culture. To take just one example, limp-wristed gestures, which to us seem feminine or, in a man, effeminate, in many parts of the Middle East are assumed to be the natural way for both men and women to move their hands.

Very little is known so far about how children learn gender signals or at what age they begin to use them. There are indications that youngsters absorb them at the age of about four in the southern United States, somewhat later in the Northeast. So it seems that the age at which the signals are learned varies even between regional subcultures. And if one looks just at the way the pelvis is held, women tip theirs up and forward and men tip back. Pelvic angle begins to be used as a gender signal, not at any particular age, but whenever the individual reaches the point where he is ready to court—

and that doesn't mean ready to copulate. Pelvic angle responds to that confusing changeover when childhood is left behind, when boys become overwhelmingly interested in girls, and girls in boys.

For the girl at adolescence there are new body movements to learn and they are interesting for what they reveal about the way the nonverbal code is taught. At puberty a girl may very quickly grow adult-sized breasts; then she has to learn what to do with them. Should she curl around them? Should she thrust them forward provocatively? Nobody will advise her in so many words. Her mother won't say to her, "Look, lift your breasts up two inches and put a little more tension on your shoulders. Don't be too provocative but stay on the market."

However, if she slumps her mother may say, irritably, "Fix your hair." And if she errs in the other direction, she may be told that her dress is too tight, or simply that she looks like a hussy. Even these lessons in body movement are more direct than the way smaller children learn.

It was the anthropologist Margaret Mead in 1935 who first pointed out in her book *Sex and Temperament in Three Primitive Societies* that many of our assumptions about masculinity and femininity are culturally shaped. Within an area of just a hundred miles, Dr. Mead found three very different tribes: one in which both sexes were aggressive and fierce; one in which both were gentle and nurturant; and one in which it was the males who were catty, arranged their hair in curls, and went shopping, while the females were "energetic, managerial, unadorned." Dr. Mead believes that there *are* sex differences, but that these basic tendencies can be overpowered by learning. She points out that "human culture can impart either congenial or uncongenial patterns of behavior."

Anthropologist Ray Birdwhistell calls *Sex and Temperament* "one of the most important things ever done in anthropology." If it produced no lasting changes in our thinking about male and female, that was, he says, because it was much too frightening for those people who believed—as most people still do—that the sexual aspects of personality are all a matter of hormones.

Professor Birdwhistell himself is the father of the young science of kinesics. It is his work on gender signals that has provided the proof that masculine and feminine body movements are programmed not by biology but by culture, and are learned in childhood. His conclusions are based on years of painstaking film analysis done at a specially equipped lab in Philadelphia.

Americans have strong feelings about gender and body motion. When we watch an Englishman or a Latin male cross his legs, for example, we sometimes feel momentarily uneasy. Though we couldn't say why, the gesture strikes us as effeminate. Few of us are consciously aware that the American male generally crosses his legs with knees somewhat spread or perhaps with one ankle propped on the other knee, while English and Latin men are apt to hold their legs and feet more or less parallel, as do American females.

These are not just body conventions, they are body prejudices. An American man has only to try to assume the posture the American woman takes when sending gender signals to learn how awkward and *wrong* it feels: legs close together, pelvis tipped forward and up, arms snug against the upper body and swinging, when she walks, only from the elbows down. And an American woman is uncomfortable if she tries the male posture: thighs somewhat apart—say, ten to fifteen degrees—and pelvis rolled back, arms held slightly away from the body and swinging from the shoulder. These different body styles are not dictated by anatomy—by women's broader hips, for example—for if they were they would be universal. Men in Eastern Europe walk with legs close together, and in the Far East, men may hold their upper arms against their bodies, any arm swing beginning below the elbow.

Even the way we move our eyelids is a culturally prescribed gender signal. A quick blink is masculine to Americans. A man who closes his lids slowly, even langorously, perhaps allowing them to remain closed for an instant while his eyeballs move visibly beneath the lids, strikes us as either effeminate or seductive, unless he is obviously very sleepy or in distress. Yet in Arab countries this is the way men normally close their eyes.

Do humans send gender signals constantly or only now and then? Obviously, American men don't always stand with thighs ten to fifteen degrees apart and pelvises rolled back. Gender signals are emphasized in some situations, de-emphasized in others. Nor are they necessarily a sign of sexual attraction. It is true that they are often an element in courtship, but they also appear in non-courtship situations. A great deal of gender signaling related to who gets up to do the dishes and who does not, how people behave in public, to something as simple as who goes through a door first, goes on between male and female in everyday situations where sexual attraction is quite irrelevant.

Americans, of course, are not the only ones to differentiate between male and female styles of movement. Birdwhistell has studied gender signals in seven very different cultures—Kutenai, Hopi, upper-class French, upper- and working-class British, Lebanese, and Hokka Chinese—and in each has found that not only can people easily point out some gestures that are "masculine" and some that are "feminine" but that on the basis of these gestures they distinguish masculine females and feminine males. It seems obvious, then, that gender signals must have developed in these (and perhaps all) cultures in response to a very basic human need—to be able to tell male from female.

In some animal species, male and female look so much alike that it seems remarkable that the animals themselves can spot the difference. The phenomenon is called unimorphy, and humans are more unimorphic than one might think. If we look at any of the secondary sexual characteristics—breast size, body shape, distribution of hair, deep or high voice, and so on—we find a great deal of overlap between human males and females. There are women with small breasts and men with large ones, women with facial hair and nearly beardless men, women with contralto voices and men who are high tenors. Humans tell the difference between male and female not by any single visible sex characteristic but by the sum of all of them, *plus* the fact that men and women move in distinctively different ways. We are helped along, of course, by conventions about dress and hair style, and the fact that men and women usually do dress differently suggests that we may need some help. But styles of dress change rapidly and gender signals don't. Gender signals, then, function as tertiary sexual characteristics: they back up the secondary characteristics and so make life a little less complicated.

On the basis of his studies of gender, Birdwhistell refutes several popular theories about human sexuality. For example, many people believe they can spot a homosexual by the way he looks—meaning by the way he moves and holds his body. But kinesicists have been unable to find any signals, masculine or feminine, which are in themselves an indication of homosexual or heterosexual commitment. Since there are no innately feminine movements, homosexuals obviously are not bound to move in "feminine" ways. A homosexual may signal that he wants to be considered a homosexual but in certain situations a man may use feminine gestures simply because he wants to keep women away—for whatever reason—and he has hit on a way to do it that is subtle but definitely offputting. On the other hand, the man who quite emphatically sends male gender signals may also succeed in driving women away. If he signals in an inappropriate situation—for example, while a woman's husband is present—he can make it impossible for her to respond without losing face.

Among women the one most determinedly feminine and sexy is often the least responsive to any real, personal approach. Birdwhistell has found a difference between a sexy woman and a sexual woman, a difference that is not hard to spot at practically any cocktail party. The sexual woman may start the evening standing on the sidelines looking uninteresting; but when she gets into conversation with a man she likes, her face and the whole way she holds her body change. A man who is aware of the change may feel that in some mysterious way *he* has made her beautiful.

The sexy woman, on the other hand, is the one in the low-cut dress who is surrounded by men. But the men she is surrounded by are men who do not really like women and are there because it is the safest spot in the room; the sexy woman is so busy sending signals that insist "I am a woman. I am a woman. I am a woman" that she demands nothing of the men she is with except their undivided attention, since she is too busy playing a part to have any real interest in them. Essentially, she is a tragic figure. Probably she was once a little girl who learned to be cute and pretty to please parents who used her as a showpiece, which taught her at the same time that people often treat each other as possessions. When she grew older, she began to be approached by men who did not *like* women. Because they needed to prove that they were men, they used her simply as what the feminists call a sexual object. In the end she becomes a brittle, anxious woman who presents a very simple picture of herself and sells a very simple commodity. She may even say, "Men are only interested in one thing." But that may actually be all she can offer; she has never learned to respond or to exchange with another human being.

"Communication," Birdwhistell summed up, "isn't like a sending set and a receiver. It's a negotiation between two people, a creative act. It's not measured by the fact that you get precisely what I say, but that you contribute your part to it, that both of us change by the act. And then when we do communicate, we're an interacting and reacting, beautifully integrated system."

And that, of course, is what gender signals are all about. They're a very basic and sensitive exchange between people—a way you affirm your sexual identity and at the same time respond to others.

3 | Courting Behaviors

We all know so much more than we think we know—this is one of the overwhelming truths brought home to anyone who studies nonverbal communication.

For example, every woman knows how to respond in a courtship situation to an attractive man. She knows how to cool off a relationship and how to encourage one, and how to manage her own behavior so that it has no sexual overtones at all. Most women can't say exactly how they do these things. Many aren't even aware that the technique is largely nonverbal, though in courtship the nonverbal cues are so persuasive that they can turn a comment about the weather into a seductive invitation.

Pioneering studies on nonverbal communication in courtship have been done by the kinesicists, chiefly by Dr. Albert Scheflen, working with Ray Birdwhistell.

In analyzing films of courtship, Scheflen has docu-

mented the fact that love *does* sometimes make a woman—or a man—beautiful, and has even pinned down in
detail just how this happens.

A woman, for example, becomes briefly beautiful
when an emotional response, such as sexual attraction,
triggers subtle changes in her body. In their deliberately
dry way, the kinesicists speak of the whole delightful
phenomenon as coming into a state of "high courtship
readiness."

In part, this readiness is a matter of heightened
muscle tone: muscles seem to snap to attention so that
the whole body is suddenly alerted. In the face, lines that
formerly sagged no longer do, and even bags under the
eyes are partially smoothed away. The eyes shine, the
skin may flush or grow pale, the lower lip swells softly.
The individual who is given to slumping may straighten
up, pot bellies miraculously diminish, and leg muscles
tighten—an effect often mimicked in cheesecake photographs. Body odor may change also, and some women
believe that even their hair texture changes. And the
extraordinary thing is that an individual can react in all
these ways and not be in the least aware of it.

Couples on the verge of courting also go in for
grooming and preening. Women play with their hair, or
sketchily tidy their clothing; a man may pass a hand over
his hair, straighten his socks, fiddle with his tie. Usually,
these are token gestures, done automatically and almost
unconsciously.

As courtship progresses, the signs are obvious: flirtatious glances and long looks into one another's eyes. But
there are also less obvious clues. Courting couples face
each other squarely—they seldom turn their bodies
aside. And they are apt to lean toward one another and
extend an arm or leg as if to block off outsiders. When
talking to a third person, if they are side by side, they
may leave their upper bodies politely open to view—

arms down or out or resting on chair arms, but not folded across the chest; but at the same time they'll form a closed circle with their legs—knees crossed from the outer sides in, so that toe tips almost meet. People often dramatize a relationship with their bodies in this way, building a barricade with arms or legs. Sometimes a couple will go in for surrogate touching—in a restaurant a woman may run a fingertip slowly and delicately around the rim of a glass, or gently trace patterns on the tablecloth. Sometimes women assume provocative postures. A woman may cross her legs, slightly exposing one thigh; she may prop a hand saucily on one hip and thrust her breasts forward; or she may sit and slowly, absent-mindedly, stroke her own thigh or wrist. Courting couples also cock their heads and use gender signals such as pelvic tilt. Palming is the subtlest signal of all. Most Anglo-Saxon women habitually hold their hands curled and show only a rare flash of palm. Yet in courting, women palm all over the place. Even gestures ordinarily done palm in, such as smoking or covering a cough, in courting may be made palm out.

Because most of us, when we think of courtship, think first of internal sensations—a feeling of excitement that's decidedly a visceral response—all this is rather like reading about cardboard people. But as good behaviorists, kinesicists limit themselves to studying behavior and refuse to speculate about feelings, on the grounds that feelings can't be measured scientifically—in fact they can't even be identified with certainty.

But obviously the feelings are there. In high courtship readiness, for example, one would feel alert, alive, attracted. Grooming and preening, far from being a serious attempt to improve the appearance, are probably done out of a sudden surge of self-awareness. Surrogate touching derives from that rather delicious conflict between the desire to touch and the feeling that, really, perhaps one ought not to—a conflict often carried on at a subconscious level. Pelvic tilt can be a particularly subtle and virtually automated signal—to the point that a woman walking down the street may be startled to feel her own pelvis register a reaction when she passes an attractive man. Of course, the same thing can happen to a man.

Palming is also an unconscious gesture. It's a temptation to derive a cheap rule from this and say that when a woman shows her palm to a man she's courting him whether she knows it or not. Sometimes that's true, but palming is also a gesture of greeting, so unless it occurs in the courtship context, combined with other courting behavior, it may not be related to sex at all. In any case, it usually happens so fleetingly that it's hard for an untrained eye to pick it up. I have never succeeded in seeing it myself, except a few times when it was pointed out to me in films run in slow motion. Then it was obvious: in the space of a few seconds, in the course of a casual arm motion, the palm would be presented, open and faced toward the other person in a gesture curiously defenseless and appealing. In real life, one is most apt to notice palming when it *doesn't* occur—at a party, for example, when the hostess greets all her guests palm out except one, to whom she presents the back of her hand. Predictably, this will be the one guest she really doesn't like. (Failure to palm is recognized in the popular idiom when a man snarls, "I'll give you the back of my hand.")

The studies of courtship done so far are fascinating in their detail, and, because of that detail, they present a certain source of temptation to the reader, to fake it. A young woman I know had a good male friend but decided that she wanted to be more than just good friends. She wondered if she could get the idea across to him by faking some of the subtler courting behaviors. But the trouble with counterfeiting is that, unless you're a consummate actor, you come across as calculating, dissociated, or just plain awkward, because one element in the body message will almost certainly be an intimation that something, somewhere, is not altogether right.

One of the problems of trying to interpret nonverbal behavior is the amazing complexity of human communication. An excellent illustration of this complexity is to be found in Dr. Scheflen's studies of quasi-courtship: behavior that is curiously like courtship but that doesn't mean the same thing at all.

While working with films of psychotherapists and their patients, Dr. Scheflen discovered that there were courtship sequences in every single film. So he investigated nontherapy situations too, and learned to his surprise that, at least in middle-class America, courtship is apt to happen in practically any situation: at cocktail parties and business meetings, between parent and child, teacher and student, doctor and patient—even between men and men, and between women and women, with no obvious homosexual overtones. People, alive, alert, standing close together, exchanging long looks, palming, preening—to all intents and purposes, courting: one must either conclude that sex is all around us and that Americans court whenever they get together, or that these courtship sequences aren't quite what they seem, that there's some kind of qualifying behavior tacked on so that all concerned will know that seduction isn't involved.

Close examination of the films proved that the qualifiers were there, that this was definitely courtship with a difference. Sometimes the difference was obvious, and expressed verbally. One person might say in so many words that courtship was not intended or appropriate, or might refer to other people present or to an absent husband or wife. Or the topic of conversation might

simply be a totally nonsexual one. Sometimes the qualifier was more subtle. Both people might face one another, but with bodies turned slightly aside; or one or the
other might extend an arm or leg as if to include a third
person. Sometimes both would keep glancing about the
room or speak in voices a shade too loud for an intimate
conversation. Or a man might talk about love and sex but
in a matter-of-fact tone of voice, leaning back in his chair
and smiling with his lips but not with his eyes. In the
American middle class, children learn the quasi-courting
sequence, qualifiers and all, in relationships with parents,
relatives, and teachers, long before they learn to strip
away the qualifiers for the real thing.

This not-quite-courtship cannot be taken as a sign
that, though sex may be impossible, both parties have a
yen for it. In fact, it seems to be a means to entirely
different ends. Time and again in the filmed psychotherapy sessions observed by Dr. Scheflen, it was used as a
way to catch the attention of someone who seemed about
to drop out of the interaction. In one film of family
therapy, the daughter at first showed signs of high
courtship readiness, obviously reacting to the therapist.
When he studiously avoided looking at her or talking to
her, she lost all interest in the proceedings. Soon two of
the other children, who seemed always to follow her
lead, began to withdraw too. The therapist, in danger of
losing contact with half the family group and trapped for
the moment in conversation with the father, began a
quasi-courting sequence: he locked eyes with the girl and
for a moment they dragged on their cigarettes in perfect
synchrony. Soon, apparently becoming uncomfortable,
the girl turned her head away sharply and placed her arm
across her lap as a barrier. But after that she was no
longer withdrawn from the group.

Actual courting behavior can be seen in another of
Scheflen's therapy films. A psychiatrist was interviewing

a family—mother, father, daughter, grandmother—for the first time. Eleven times in just twenty minutes, the same revealing sequence took place. The therapist would become involved in conversation with either the daughter or the grandmother; the mother would immediately begin courting behavior. Delicately crossing her ankles and extending her legs, she would place one hand on her hip and lean forward. Each time the therapist responded with tie-preening or some other grooming gesture and turned to ask her a question. Whereupon the father would begin to jiggle one foot nervously and immediately the daughter and grandmother, who were seated on either side of the mother, would cross their knees so that their toe tips almost met in front of the mother, effectively boxing her in. As soon as this happened the mother would begin to "decourt": she lost all her alert muscle tone and slumped back in her chair, looking so withdrawn that to the psychiatric eye she seemed autistic.

Though the mother in this film might have been using quasi-courtship to catch the therapist's attention, that seems unlikely, since she didn't show any of the qualifying behaviors, and since her family reacted as if this were the real thing—a seductive invitation. As it turned out, the mother's seductive behavior *was* a problem for this family. Dr. Scheflen has said that family signal systems such as those revealed in this film sequence are common—in fact, he believes that all families have them, sharing a whole vocabulary of gestures at some subconscious level. I imagine that the daughter and the grandmother might have been only faintly aware of the father's disquiet, but when he did his foot wiggle they reacted together immediately.

Quasi-courtship also occurs in situations where there's gender confusion. When a woman becomes aggressive or domineering, behaving in a way our culture insists is inappropriate for her sex, a man will sometimes quasi-court her as a kind of reminder. When a man behaves passively, a woman may try out quasi-courtship to discourage his supposedly feminine behavior.

Sometimes quasi-courting and decourting seem to work together as a kind of thermostatic device to maintain group morale. Almost everyone has seen a dull party or a dull business meeting come alive with the arrival of just one vividly attractive person. Others in the room immediately become more animated and themselves more attractive. In a situation like this, a body-motion analysis would reveal that the new arrival triggered whole sequences of quasi-courtship. On the other hand, if one member of the group quasi-courts too enthusiastically, raising the general level of intimacy and excitement above what is mutually acceptable, others in the group will decourt, apparently trying to defuse the situation.

Quasi-courtship, then, is far from being simply an abortive attempt by A to get B into bed. I think it may be related to moments of real rapport and to a feeling, within the individual, of alertness, well-being, even excitement—a feeling that takes on quite a different quality when sexual attraction *is* involved.

Scheflen's courtship studies were of the American middle class. What evidence there is, and there isn't much, suggests that not only are courting behaviors subtly different elsewhere, but that there are regional differences even within the United States. The flirtatious behavior that's perfectly appropriate at a middle-class cocktail party in the city or suburbs may not go down at all well at a similar party in a small town, a rural area, or a working-class neighborhood. Middle-class quasi-courtship can appear confusing or even threatening in a working-class group, where a courtship qualifier is more apt to come in the form of a broad burlesque of courtship than as one of the subtler signals.

But it seems that there *are* some courting behaviors that are the same all over the world. The Austrian ethologist Irenäus Eibl-Eibesfeldt, once a student and now a colleague of Konrad Lorenz, has studied flirting in six cultures and found it similar in many of its details. He filmed it using a two-man team, one man to operate the camera and the other to smile and nod at girls. And girls in Samoa, Papua, France, Japan, and Africa, and Indian girls in South America, all went through the same little kinesic dance in response: a smile, a quick, quirky lift of the eyebrows—a "yes" reaction—followed by a turning away, with head turned aside and sometimes lowered, eyes lowered, eyelids dropped. Often, the girl would cover her face with one hand and smile or laugh with embarrassment. Sometimes, she would continue looking at the man from the corners of her eyes, or she would look at him before looking away quickly.

A stage-by-stage analysis of human courtship, begun recently by Dr. Adam Kendon, a psychologist who has worked with Scheflen, has turned up other possibly universal features that can also be seen in animal courtship. Kendon's study, using films of couples that were taken in public parks, indicates that, for the woman, courtship combines two different elements. First, she shows off her sexuality to attract the man, then she reassures him with childlike behavior—coy looks, cocked head, and soft, babyish gestures. The man, in turn, demonstrates his male prowess, perhaps by standing tall and gesturing aggressively, and also reassures by becoming somewhat childlike.

The parallel animal behavior arises from the actual physical danger involved in the courtship situation among animals. The male of the species risks an ill-tempered attack if the female isn't feeling receptive, and when it's the female who makes the first approach, she sometimes takes a beating before the male is reassured, by the very fact that she doesn't fight back, that she's not a threat. So animal courtship also generally has two stages: first the individual must attract a sexual partner; then it must overcome the other's fear of close contact. Imitations of the young are sometimes used to reassure. The male woodpecker finch may invite the female into his nest by mimicking the gestures of a nestling begging for food. Male hamsters when courting imitate the baby hamster's call.

Though few humans ever approach courtship with the idea that they may be risking life and limb, there are definite emotional risks involved; and the coy, childlike behavior recorded by the camera is certainly familiar. Dr. Kendon recalls that he once described his theory on courtship to a feminist, who thought about it for a while and then said, "You may be right, but if it's so it's got to change. That coyness isn't my idea of the new woman." But if Kendon *is* right about the courtship formula, it can't change, because if a woman—or a man—fails either to attract or to reassure, there will be no courtship at all.

Where courtship is concerned, too much conscious knowledge can be an uncomfortable thing. I discovered this one evening at a cocktail party when I suddenly became overwhelmingly aware of the fact that I was, as the kinesicists might put it, in a state of high courtship readiness: my eyes were bright, my face was flushed, my lower lip was slightly swollen, and I was absently stroking my own hair. For just a minute or two the knowledge was paralyzing. But once over that first acute self-consciousness, I discovered that courtship, or quasi-courtship, was going on all around me. After that, I could relax and enjoy—watching, behaving, feeling—in a new and different way.

4 | The Silent, Celluloid World of Kinesics

Visually, the film is as bland as pablum: from an impersonal distance the camera has recorded four people, sitting and endlessly talking. The occasion is a psychotherapy session. The two men are psychiatrists who work together as a team, and the two women are mother and daughter. The daughter is schizophrenic.

As the film is run through in silent slow motion, a pattern becomes clear. Every few minutes the daughter crosses her legs seductively, exposing rather a lot of thigh, and turns to the older of the two psychiatrists in such a way that one breast is thrust toward him—clearly, courtship behavior. Each time she does this, her mother makes a particular gesture: she sweeps the side of an index finger across her nostrils. Immediately, the girl uncrosses her legs and withdraws from conversation with the man. Sometimes the mother simply crosses her ankles in a particular way, with or without the nose wipe. The effect on her daughter is the same.

Several times the mother seems about to move toward an alliance with one of the psychiatrists. Each time the daughter reacts dramatically, sprawling in her chair or suddenly standing up with a shocked expression on her face. Without saying a word, and without being really conscious of what they're doing, the two women monitor each other's behavior and so defend and preserve their own one-to-one relationship.

As the session wears on, though, there are variations in the pattern. The girl crosses her legs and begins her seductive bid for the older man's attention, but now the young psychiatrist, who has been conversationally allied with the mother, does the nose wipe. It seems he has learned the monitoring signal, unawares. Furthermore, the older psychiatrist has, throughout the session, paused to light or tamp his pipe whenever he was about to turn his attention to the girl; but now he has only to begin the pipe-lighting ritual and the mother immediately does her nose wipe.

Years of studying films such as this one have led a pioneering kinesicist, Ray Birdwhistell, to conclude that much of the real, bedrock business of human communication is carried out on a level below consciousness at which words are only indirectly relevant. He estimates that no more than thirty-five percent of the social meaning in any conversation is embedded in the words that are spoken.

There are times when the scientist is at least as fascinating as the science, times when to an extraordinary degree the man's own view of the human condition shapes and informs his work. This is true of kinesics, which is very much the brain child of one man—Ray Birdwhistell—and the history of kinesics is primarily the history of the development of his thought.

Birdwhistell first conceived an interest in body motion in 1946, when he was doing an anthropological field study in western Canada and was living among the Kutenai Indians. It struck him then that the Indians looked entirely different when speaking English than they did when speaking Kutenai. Their smiles, head nods, movements of the eyebrows, all changed.

"It was something that haunted me after I left there," he said.

It seems that some people are bilingual in body language as well as in spoken language. Films exist showing New York's famous mayor, Fiorello La-Guardia, politicking in English, Yiddish, and Italian. With the sound switched off, it's easy to tell just from the Little Flower's gestures which language he was speaking. A Frenchman not only speaks but gestures in French; an American moves in a distinctively American way. An expert in kinesics can actually tell a European from an American just by the way they move their eyebrows in conversation.

In the late nineteen forties, Birdwhistell became involved in actual body-motion studies. As others have done since, he started with the idea that the really basic human emotions, such as joy, fear, or sexual attraction, must be expressed the same way in all cultures and that therefore there must be some gestures or expressions that are universal to mankind. It was a logical assumption to make—most of us simply take it for granted that men all over the world smile when they're happy, scowl when they're angry, and so on. However, as Birdwhistell says, he soon came to the conclusion that "there are no universal gestures. As far as we know, there is no single facial expression, stance, or body position which conveys the same meaning in all societies."

The word "meaning" is the crux of Birdwhistell's statement. Anatomically speaking, all men smile—to take just one familiar expression. But the meaning of smiling is different in different cultures. Even within the United States, there are high smile areas, such as the South, where people do a lot of smiling, and low smile areas where they don't—for example, New England or the even more dour western part of New York State. In the Great Lakes region, a person who does a lot of smiling may be asked what's so funny; in Georgia, someone who doesn't smile much may be asked if something is wrong. It's not that those who smile a lot are simply happier, but rather that as children all of us learn in which situations we are expected to smile and in which ones we're not expected to, and we learn differently in different parts of the country. Furthermore, Birdwhistell found, there's no such thing as a simple smile. The position of the head, the expression around the eyes, even the general body posture can be, and in fact usually are, involved in smiling. For example, a head cocked to one side can add a flirtatious air, while a smile that doesn't bring out laugh lines around the eyes or that goes with a sagging body usually seems forced.

Having written off universals, Birdwhistell turned his attention to the kinds of gestures that have a conscious, understood meaning. The salute is one good example; the hitchhiker's thumbing, another. Every culture has its own repertoire of these. An Italian, when he sees a pretty girl, may comment by tugging at one ear lobe; an Arab in the same situation will stroke his beard, while an American makes two downward, in-and-out movements with his hands as if outlining womanly curves. However, these gestures are also often used as a kind of ironic comment when the woman in question isn't at all attractive, with the irony supplied by facial expression, posture, or some other body behavior. In the same way, an experienced army private, when he salutes, can convey anything from approval to ridicule just by what he does with his face or body stance, or by the speed and duration of the arm movement, or simply by choosing to salute in a situation in which a salute isn't at all appropriate.

It was Birdwhistell's realization that even gestures such as these are only partial acts, which must be accompanied by other gestures to have meaning, that led to one of the real breakthroughs in the development of kinesics. For if gestures were rather like stem forms in language—"cept," for example, which is meaningless until you add the prefix that makes it "except"—then it seemed likely that body motion was also similar to language in other ways, and could perhaps be analyzed by a kind of systems analysis, the way linguists analyze speech.

Since 1959, Professor Birdwhistell has had his own laboratory in Philadelphia at Eastern Pennsylvania Psychiatric Institute, where he is Senior Research Scientist and Director of the Studies in Human Communication project. I interviewed him there. Because his writing is properly dense and scholarly, the man himself was a surprise: tall, tweedy, fiftyish, with an unexpectedly deep voice and the kind of face that creases easily into a smile. Colleagues call him "brilliant" and "a damn-fool genius," but many, particularly the psychologists, also complain that his work is long on theory—controversial, highly provocative theory—and short on good, solid data that other researchers can sink their professional teeth into.

"I am a question-asker, rather than an answer-giver," he has said.

The Philadelphia lab is more like a suburban office building than a layman's idea of a scientist's laboratory. There are quiet corridors, sunny offices—and storerooms stocked with cinematic paraphernalia. There might be no kinesics without the movie camera or the slow-motion analyzer, a projector that can be run at any speed, enabling the viewer to examine and record a film frame by frame.

As Birdwhistell discovered by watching his films, the analogy between kinesics and language holds up nicely. Just as speech can be broken down into sounds, words, sentences, paragraphs, and so on, there are similar units in kinesics. The smallest one is the kine, a mere twitch, the slightest perceptible movement. Above that are the larger and more significant movements called kinemes, and they have a meaning when taken in context. Americans have only fifty or sixty kinemes for the whole body, including about thirty-three for the face and head. These last include four eyebrow positions (lifted, lowered, knit, and single-brow movement), four eyelid positions, seven mouth positions, three ways to nod the head (single, double, and triple nods), and so on. Obviously, these represent only a tiny fraction of the movements of which the face and head are capable. In fact, out of the truly astronomical number of movements that are anatomically possible for the human body, each culture attaches meaning to only a few.

Kinemes are sometimes interchangeable: one can be substituted for another without altering the meaning. Take eyebrows—a simple bilateral eyebrow lift often expresses doubt or accompanies a question; but it can also be used to stress a word within a sentence.

Because human movement patterns are so complex, they can't be analyzed on sight; they must first be transcribed, a problem that has plagued most students of communication. Birdwhistell solved it years ago by inventing his own ingenious shorthand system, one that has been adapted and used by some other scientists since.

For every kine, Birdwhistell conceived a shorthand symbol. The direction of movement of each kine is recorded by still another set of symbols. The notations are simple and often graphic: for example, a cocked head is indicated by a capital H (for head) with a line drawn diagonally through it. A "toothy" smile is a crescent with teeth blocked in, and for hunched shoulders the symbol is a capital T with the T-bar bent gently upward at each end, like the roof of a pagoda.

This peculiar shorthand is the key to the research technique called microanalysis, which is itself an incredibly painstaking, time-consuming procedure. At normal speed most films skim past at the rate of twenty-four frames per second. Therefore, to do microanalysis the researcher must record everything that goes on—every eyebrow lift, every hand motion and body shift—in twenty-four frames for each second of film. He makes this record, using the notation system, on huge sheets of graph paper, and the result looks a bit like a conductor's orchestral score. Birdwhistell told me that it takes him an hour to analyze one second of film, and commented, "I noticed once that in one afternoon I looked at two and a half seconds of film one thousand and eight times."

When he has finished his paperwork, Birdwhistell checks it over for regularities, the patterns that recur again and again. They aren't hard to find. In twenty minutes of film, the same sequences repeat themselves literally hundreds of times. One of the startling things about body movement is just how repetitious it is.

The meaning of the message is always embedded in the context and never in any isolated body movement. For example, from the film described at the beginning of this chapter one might be tempted into the generalization that a nose wipe always signifies disapproval. The truth is that it may or may not. However, it's clear that in this particular context that's just how it can be interpreted—in the film it was part of a pattern that occurred over and over again: the daughter would make a seductive move; the mother would wipe her nose; the daughter would withdraw.

Because meaning is to be found always and only in terms of the context, we will never have a reliable dictionary of unconscious gestures. We'll never be able to say, that when a woman sits with arms folded and legs tightly crossed she is always signaling that she's unapproachable. Often that's true—but to be sure of it one has to look at the context, at what else she does with her body, what other people are around, and so on.

Birdwhistell's findings, after years of kinesics research, run the gamut from the discovery of whole categories of minute movements that are tied into the speech stream to wide-ranging observations on psychiatry, gender signals, and human relationships in general. He learned, for example, that there are minimovements as inseparable from speech as the punctuation is from a written sentence. For example, he has found that Americans are apt to end a statement with a droop of the head or hand or a lowering of the eyelids, while they wind up a question with a lift of the hand, a tilt of the chin, or a widening of the eyes.

Certain words and phrases are usually accompanied by "markers," particular small movements of the head, eyes, hands, fingers, or shoulders. With the pronouns "I," "me," "we," and "us," as well as with words such as "this" and "here," a hand marker would be a motion toward the speaker's body. For the plural pronouns, the gesture ends with a little, pluralizing, sideways sweep. If the shoulders were used instead, they would be squeezed or hunched in the direction of an imaginary vertical line through the center of the body. With pronouns such as "you," "they," and "that" the marker is away from that imaginary midline. With future tense verbs, there's a marker movement forward; with the past tense, it's backward. All this seems so logical to Americans that it's a surprise to learn that other peoples—for example, some American Indians—sometimes find these markers confusing or even insulting when they are combined with their language.

Also necessary to American English is the kinesic

stress system, which helps clear up verbal ambiguities. It's not just vocal stress that tells us, when someone uses the phrase "hot dog," whether he means an overheated canine or something to eat or is simply exclaiming. Some small body motion must be made as well—a kind of "body English" done with tiny head nods, hand sweeps, eye blinks, small lip movements, chin thrusts, shoulder nods and sweeps, hand and finger movements, leg and foot shifts, and thrusts of the chest area.

Another important finding corroborated by films is that sometimes nonverbal behavior contradicts what is said instead of underlining it. A man who is basically a passive little guy—what Birdwhistell calls a "masculinoid"—will sometimes throw all the authoritativeness he can muster into what he says and into tone of voice, while in the slumped way he holds his body, the hesitancy of his gestures, he remains as ineffectual as ever. And we sometimes see couples going through a whole repertoire of intimate, courting behavior while carrying on an intellectual discussion about books or while talking about how faithful they've always been to their respective spouses. Conversely, a highly sexed dialogue is sometimes not accompanied by any courting behavior at all. In a case like this, people tend to believe the nonverbal component since it's less likely to be under conscious control.

Inevitably, kinesics research raises certain questions. How can a body movement communicate when it's so small and unobtrusive that it passes unnoticed in everyday life and only seems significant in a slow-motion replay? Isn't such a replay a distortion of real life, and isn't it possible that kinesicists are inferring body messages that just aren't there?

It is difficult to believe that people can send and receive messages, even nonverbal ones, without being at all aware that they are doing it. But it can hardly be a coincidence when a behavior sequence is repeated over and over again, as it was in the nose-wipe film, and always with the same result. Perhaps there is a partial biological explanation in the mental phenomenon of attention.

Scientists are still trying to understand attention, the filter system in the human brain stem that selects from the whole dizzy kaleidoscope of incoming sensations— sights, sounds, and so on—the particular ones the individual will pay attention to, think about, and perhaps act upon. Obviously we see and hear much more than we "absorb"—in the sense of being consciously aware of it. Stop right now for a moment to register all the sounds you have been shutting out as you read this; all the sights you have been blocking that are nevertheless available to your peripheral vision; all the sensations—of chair seat against backside and feet against floor—that you have been ignoring. The signals we're unaware of, the ones that don't claim our attention, apparently are either weakened by the filter or absorbed but not analyzed. But they do have their impact at some subliminal level, and communication research makes this point again and again.

Birdwhistell summed up his particular view of human communication for me this way:

> Years ago, I started with the question: How do body motions flesh out words? Now I ask instead: When is it appropriate to use words? They're very appropriate to teach or to talk on the telephone, but you and I are communicating on several levels right now and on only one or two of them have words any relevance whatsoever. These days I put it another way: Man is a multisensorial being. Occasionally, he verbalizes.

5 The Body Is the Message

One of the more startling theories put forward by communication experts is the notion that sometimes the body itself communicates—and not only by the way it moves or the postures it assumes. There can also be a message in the very shape of the body and even in the way the features of the face are arranged, according to Ray Birdwhistell, who believes that physical appearance is often culturally programmed.

Birdwhistell believes that we learn our looks—we're not born with them. When a baby is small, his features are generally soft and unformed: a blob of a nose above a small, urgent, almost lipless mouth, a face that's all cheeks and eyes with the potential to become almost anything. Even eyebrows are subject to change, for they can be very mobile and only gradually become set at a certain distance above the eyes. Just how far above is something the baby learns from those around him, family and friends. Birdwhistell says that this helps to explain why the people of some regions look so much alike, when it can't be a matter of shared genes. Eyebrow level can be a very distinctive characteristic. There are people who are beetle browed, while others—some upper-class Englishmen, for example—wear their eyebrows so far above their eyes that, to Americans, they look perpetually surprised.

Scalp placement, too, is set not at birth but later, which means that to some extent high foreheads are also learned. In general, the upper part of the head matures earlier than the lower part. The nasal septum rises some time between the ages of nine and eleven, and because humans have two sets of teeth—milk teeth and permanent ones—the mouth takes shape still later, often not until after puberty.

Just as people learn how to carry their bodies, they learn how to carry their mouths, and how they carry them has a great deal to do with the way they look. Birdwhistell likes to point out that his own face is "rather traditional middle border state—with the heavy lower lip, the overheavy laugh lines, the bad occlusion." He does a fascinating transformation from middle-border-state mouth to thin-lipped New England style and then to the western New York State look, which has the lower lip projected slightly and carried over the upper.

Not surprisingly, he believes that husband and wife often learn to look alike and that it may even be true that dog owners sometimes come to resemble their dogs. The husband-wife resemblance isn't hard to spot at any gathering if you forget about characteristics such as hair color and look at the expression around the mouth and around the eyes.

These theories about the face are somewhat unsettling to people who like to ponder family resemblances.

They disrupt the old game of trying to decide which side of the family a child resembles, and they raise some interesting questions about *why* some children strongly resemble one parent but not the other, whenever the likeness isn't really a matter of bone structure. But they also explain how it happens that children who are adopted often grow up to look so much like their acquired parents. Adoption agencies do try to match up physical appearances, but sometimes it seems that they succeed beyond anybody's wildest dreams.

The idea that husband and wife can grow to look alike also raises some interesting questions. I was once at a party with five couples, all of whom had been married for about fifteen years. With four of the couples there was a striking resemblance between husband and wife; with the fifth, there was none, and I couldn't help wondering why. Is a strong resemblance a sign of good rapport, or weak character, or something else entirely?

In any case, that's not the kind of question the kinesicists usually ask. The real point is that humans are enormously imitative and marvelously sensitive to the body signals of others—communication research demonstrates this again and again.

Not only do we learn our faces, but Birdwhistell believes that beauty and ugliness, gracefulness and awkwardness are also learned. He has noticed that French children, for example, no matter how beautiful they are when they're younger, have a way of becoming temporarily quite unattractive at the age of about seven. Japanese children are often metamorphosed from tender little dolls into older youngsters who are somehow shrivelled and angry looking. Perhaps in each culture the people simply expect that at certain ages children will become, for a time, unattractive.

It's hard to believe that something as concretely

physical as a child's appearance can be culturally determined. But here the terms *beauty* and *ugliness* don't refer just to the shape of a face or to the possession of a classic profile. They're primarily a way of holding and moving the body and also a way of holding the face, for face muscles can be alert, slack, or grimly clenched. These things aren't biological givens, they're responses —as the kinesics studies of courting and decourting indicate: responses to other people, to inner needs, and on another, more long-term level in time, to cultural expectations.

Society also tells us who can be graceful and who can't be, which is very much part of the beauty syndrome. Just a generation ago a boy who was six foot one was considered to be uncomfortably tall and expected to be awkward. But expectations have changed and nowadays tall men are allowed to be graceful. Among women, short-boned girls generally mature early and, learning in their teens how to be small and cute, may feel quite mature at a time when their taller girl friends are still lanky and awkward and described as young for their age. Surprisingly often, the tall girl becomes quite beautiful in her late twenties or early thirties, just when the short girl is running into trouble because her only alternatives—in terms of what the society expects of her—are to try to go on looking eighteen or nineteen and cute, or to give in to dumpiness and early middle age.

The shape of the body is another physical characteristic that may be culturally programmed. Body shape is a matter of style, really, and styles change. The slender look that Birdwhistell calls "Ivy League linear" spread during the last twenty-five years in our culture. What happened to the female figure was that the nineteenth-century style—which we would regard as fat—was replaced by the boy-girl of the twenties, which was replaced in turn by the boy-girl plus breasts of the sixties. For men, the current body style is still more linear; even the hippie look is remarkably similar.

> It's bent over and with lots of hair, but it has the same extreme linearity [Birdwhistell explained]. It's essentially a nine-year-old look but doing all the things Mother told them not to do: the dirty clothes, the sag, the face in droop, and the clean decent smile. And it isn't really a mixing up of male and female, but a prepubertal look. It says, "we are pre- the period where it counts," rather than saying that the sex differences don't count. Of course, I'm stereotyping. I have to. These are kids who care about things or who are rebelling, but they're in uniform and they pay for the uniform with a degree of conformity greater than the conformity they despise in their elders.

The faces we learn and the way we present our bodies carry not just the signature of our culture, they're our own signatures as well. They are one way we tell society whether to reward us or not. The attractive, vivacious child gets more attention and opportunities than the unattractive one. But not everyone wants to be a leader, and success, because it generally entails new responsibilities, actually frightens many people. By being somewhat ugly, people reduce their responsibilities. They can also punish themselves, their parents, their husbands or wives. Obesity, for instance, can be self-punishment; it can also be a way to insulate oneself against sexual approaches—and some people feel more confident, more imposing, when they're bigger.

A message about looks is a message not just about the individual but also about what he is saying. A fiery political speech delivered by a man with dull eyes, a sagging face, and a drooping body, would be uninteresting to listen to—the speaker would be saying with his body there's no need to pay attention, because I have nothing really interesting to say. Some political sooth-sayers believe that in the famous Kennedy-Nixon TV debate in 1960, the contrast between Kennedy's obvious vitality and Nixon's fatigue (plus his customary wooden-ness) was more important than anything either man said.

Birdwhistell's beauty and ugliness studies, his asser-tion that we learn our looks, constitute a whole new way of thinking about appearance. Beauty becomes some-thing rather different when you accept the fact that how you look is a message you send. That message may be dictated partly by society, but it can't be written off, as most of us assume it can be, as just a matter of heredity and luck.

6 | Greetings from a Very Old Primate

In the infancy of the human race, before the evolution of language, man communicated the only way he could—nonverbally. Animals still communicate without words and many of them are able to exchange information to a greater extent than was thought possible just a few years ago. In some ways, the nonverbal behavior of humans is strikingly similar to the necessarily nonverbal behavior of animals, particularly of the other primates. We still communicate some of the same things that animals do, and in much the same ways—but since the advent of words we are no longer conscious that we're doing it.

Recently, ethologists have begun to study, analyze, and compare the communication systems of men and of animals. Their methods and their findings are having more and more influence on the other scientists who study nonverbal communication. There have been suggestions, in fact, that the whole field might better be called "human ethology."

The ethologist is basically a biologist but one whose particular concern is the behavior that enables the animal to adapt to its environment—including its social environment, which means other members of the species. When the ethologist turns his attention to humans, he asks: Just how far can the behavior of man be understood as a product of the evolutionary process?

The best way to learn about the evolution of human behavior is to compare the activities of humans with those of man's closest living relatives, the monkeys and apes. We know quite a lot now about social organization among primates, their ecology, and how they communicate; surprisingly, we have very little similar information about man. His institutions, his language, his higher mental processes have all been exhaustively studied, but there is no similar body of work on how he *behaves* as he courts, mates, handles his children, and meets his fellows face-to-face.

The ethologist, in approaching human behavior, tries to describe these everyday activities. He is particularly interested in finding out which patterns of behavior are universal to mankind, for these are thought to be the oldest forms of all and possible sources of clues to the behavior patterns of early man or even of pre-man. Some facial expressions may actually be precoded in the genes which prescribe the structures of the brain and so, perhaps, the eventual behavior it directs. When behavior universal to man is also found among some of the lower primates, that's generally taken to be additional evidence of its hereditary nature. However, other universals may be dictated by man's anatomy. It has been reported, for example, that the sign-language symbol for food or for eating seems to be, universally, a hand-to-mouth gesture. But since, for all humans, hands and mouths are inevitably involved in eating, this gesture, while it may be hereditary, is at least as likely to be simply a matter of anatomy.

Recent studies on greeting patterns provide some of the most intriguing examples of the behavior men share with the apes. It seems that all wild animals greet one another, and apes do it with gestures very similar to man's. Jane Goodall, the famous ethologist who has lived for long periods of time with chimpanzees in the wild, has reported that chimps sometimes embrace and kiss, actually touching lips. They also bow and shake hands, and they've even been known to slap one another on the back in what looks to be hearty welcome.

Ethologists believe that among animals greetings often serve as an appeasement ceremony. Whenever two animals approach one another there is always the danger of physical attack, so one or both will make a gesture of appeasement, to signal that no harm is meant. Anyone who doubts that greeting serves a similar function in man might try *not* greeting friends and relations for one week. Hurt feelings, resentment, anger, blossom rapidly. When humans bow or incline their heads in greeting, these are probably submissive gestures, similar to what chimpanzees do. Bowing is found in widely different cultures, as is palm presentation, the gesture in which the palm is turned toward the one being greeted.

The Austrian ethologist Irenäus Eibl-Eibesfeldt believes that some facets of the greeting pattern may be truly universal. In every culture he has studied, friends sighting one another from a distance will smile and then, if they're in an especially good mood, do a quick lift-and-return with their eyebrows—what he calls an eyebrow flash—and nod their heads. He filmed this sequence of behavior even in Stone Age Papuans whose first contact with government patrols was so recent it was unlikely they would have had the chance to learn it.

On the other hand there are ample illustrations of greetings that differ dramatically from one culture to the next. One anthropologist, Weston La Barre, reports that among Andaman Islanders on the Gulf of Bengal, friends or relatives who haven't seen each other in several weeks will sit down together, one in the lap of the other, put their arms about each other's necks, and cry for several minutes. If the two are husband and wife, the man sits in the lap of the woman. Among the Ainu of Yezo in Japan, a man meeting his sister briefly takes her hands, then suddenly seizes her by both ears and utters the traditional Ainu cry; then they stroke one another on the face and shoulders. If that sounds a bit ridiculous, consider how the Ainu might react to the sight of two Americans, carefully brushing cheeks while they kiss the air.

How can greetings be both universal to mankind and specific to each culture? The answer becomes clear when you think of a greeting not as a single act but as a sequence of acts. The smile and eyebrow flash take place at a distance, early in the sequence, while the earpulling or cheek brushing, or whatever, happens close up. In fact, a kinesics analysis of greetings has identified five distinct, orderly stages: sighting and recognition; a distance greeting such as a wave or an eyebrow flash; the approach; a close salutation such as a kiss; and then a backing off.

Sometimes the order varies—one might sight and recognize, approach, and then wave, for example. Sometimes the individuals are already in proximity when they notice one another; still, they'll go through a little dance, making small adjustments in postures and positions during a kind of stationary approach stage. But the greeting sequence always ends with backing off, and how that is done can be significant. Both individuals may turn their bodies aside as they separate, or they may continue to face each other squarely; or else one may turn aside though the other doesn't. These small differences probably indicate just how warm the relationship is—turning aside being obviously less warm than continuing to focus on the other with the whole body. Apparently in greeting one another, people signal in small ways the kind of relationship they have had in the past, or perhaps the kind they hope to have in the future.

The analysis of greetings just described was done by Dr. Adam Kendon, a psychologist with an ethological slant on human behavior. Kendon works at Bronx State Hospital in New York, and his greetings study was done in collaboration with Dr. Andrew Ferber, a family therapist at the hospital.

Kendon cautions that this study is not "the gospel truth on greetings," since it is based on his analysis of only one film. However, the film itself is fascinating. I found that watching it and listening to Kendon describe what was happening was like observing the behavior of unfamiliar animals.

The occasion for the movie was a five-year-old's back-yard birthday party. The film shows the child's mother and father greeting guests of all ages, who arrived singly and in batches. All in all, it contained seventy separate greetings and the day I interviewed Kendon he was busy analyzing them, breaking them down into the five stages, and looking for similarities and differences from one greeting to the next.

In the first sequence Kendon showed me—run through in slow motion—the greeting stages were particularly clear. First came the sighting. A woman in a brightly flowered jumpsuit, seated under a tree, looked up, craning to see who was coming. Then she rose to her feet with a smile, but one that showed her upper teeth only. The "upper smile," as some British ethologists are now calling it, is beginning to be identified as the typical smile of greeting.

Making her approach now, the woman started up a path to meet the arriving guests. Seen in slow motion, she drifted across the ground as gently as an untethered balloon, long hair floating out behind her. Head back, she called out, "Hi!" and then lowered her head and averted her eyes. Usually, Kendon explained to me, this brief head lowering follows a distance greeting.

Coming to the spot that apparently represented to her the boundary of her territory—she stopped again and again at this particular point when going to greet guests—the woman stood and waited. As the territory owner, she maintained a fairly steady gaze, but her guests generally approached with eyes averted. When entering another's territory, Kendon told me, one seldom looks the owner directly in the eyes; that would seem too much like a challenge.

Just before reaching the hostess, one guest—a woman—dipped her head sharply, a gesture so common at this stage that Kendon has given it a name—the "pre-close-salutation-phase cut-off." Then the guest lifted one arm and placed it across her body, cocked her head, and smiled. A psychiatrist might interpret that crossed-over arm as a defensive gesture and perhaps it is. Kendon is particularly intrigued with the fact that Jane Goodall has reported an identical gesture in chimpanzees, particularly in subordinate ones as they approach or are approached by a more dominant chimp.

Then the guest extended her hand with an odd, open, palm-up motion that was, again, strikingly like the chimp handshake: the lower-status chimp holds out a limp paw in what is almost a begging gesture and the higher-status animal takes hold of the paw reassuringly.

The two women pumped hands and then finally they stepped back and both turned aside—indicating, if Kendon and Ferber are right, that theirs was not a particularly close relationship.

The film showed that the host's greeting behavior was

rather different from that of the hostess. Whereas she typically took up a stance at the edge of her territory—arms and shoulders back, head cocked, smiling—her husband advanced to greet guests with his neck extended and then raised his arms for a welcoming embrace in a very particular way—lifting them straight out to the sides, almost as if his wrists were on strings. Male guests approaching him, on the other hand, held their trunks erect, their necks were not extended, and when they brought their arms up for an embrace they lifted them straight up so that their arms were on the inside, the host's on the outside.

"So far these are just some observations we've made," Kendon explained, "but we wonder whether the host's stance is a kind of dominant-greeter's posture that we will be seeing only in males who are being greeted on their own territory." As I looked at the film, it seemed a logical conclusion to come to. The host's gesture was expansive, outgoing, as befitted a man who was solidly on his own turf. The guests' gestures were more reserved.

After the host and the various guests embraced, they backed off and one or both always looked away. Kendon calls this the cut-off and thinks it may be an equilibrium-maintaining device. Every relationship except a very new one has its own customary level of intimacy and if a greeting is more intimate than the relationship generally warrants, some kind of cutoff is needed afterward so that everything can quickly get back to normal. Perhaps that's why close-up salutations become a ritual—the handshake, the brushing of cheek against cheek that usually substitutes among Americans for a real lips-on-cheek kiss. What is ritualized loses its intimate aura and its sexual connotations.

Again and again in the greetings film the camera caught people making grooming gestures: smoothing their hair, adjusting eyeglasses or clothing. Kendon noted that this always happened just before or just after a face-to-face encounter and almost never while people were actually talking together. The other primates go in for a great deal of grooming, picking away both at themselves and at other animals. Some of this is clearly functional and meant to improve the condition of fur or skin, but mutual grooming is also a form of socializing and self-grooming is sometimes a "displacement activity." The animal, torn between attacking and running away, will sit and scratch furiously or will nervously pluck at his fur in between making threatening gestures. Human-communication experts suggest that when we scratch ourselves in public it's rarely because we itch, and the kind of cursory, public hair and body grooming that both men and women do is rarely a real attempt to tidy up. Exactly what these gestures may signify varies with the situation—grooming, for example, can be a preliminary to courtship, as we've seen—but very often it seems to reflect, as in lower primates, some inner tension that for the time being has no other outlet.

Most human encounters not only begin with a greeting, they end with a farewell of some sort. People once again come close together and then go through a parting ritual. Ethologists have suggested that, as in greeting, the purpose may be appeasement. During an encounter everyone is presumably occupied with whatever transpires, but at the moment of leaving pent-up aggression can break loose. In any case there's nothing so vulnerable as an individual in flight. In some societies, people quitting the presence of the king traditionally back from the room, bowing—and, incidentally, protecting their rears.

Humans, of course, can appease with words as well as with rituals—by what they say they reassure each other. In any case, we don't live with the sense that we're in imminent physical danger whenever we meet a fellow human being face to face. But listening to the ethologists and watching Kendon's film, one wonders whether, on some deep unconscious level, we do perhaps retain the physical caution of our primate ancestors.

Someday, a researcher may do an analysis of farewells similar to the one that's been done on greetings. It should answer some intriguing questions, such as how, in a gathering, a wife signals her husband that it's time to go home, if she can't tell him in words. I've seen women do it by moving forward onto the edges of their chairs, by gathering up belongings or resettling their clothes—in general, by briefly sketching out a bit of the departure sequence. One executive—who preferred to remain nameless—told me that he'd hit on a very simple way to bring a dull meeting to an end. He starts unobtrusively tucking away papers in his briefcase. Soon, others at the meeting also begin to shuffle papers, apparently catching the behavior from him, and the chairman, faced with what looks to be a mass urge to depart, hastily adjourns the meeting.

In their studies of small behaviors, such as greetings, ethologists are making their own distinctive contribution to nonverbal research. More than that, their work has influenced the thinking of almost every researcher in the field. Many scientists now make a habit of comparing their discoveries about human communication to animal communication.

The Human Face 7

A student nurse sits in a darkened room, watching a film that is the kind of thing nightmares are made of. On the screen a human being, horribly burned on the face and entire body, stands clenched in agony while layers of his skin are painfully stripped away.

The girl is not quite alone in her ordeal. Another woman, an interviewer, is in the room with her, sitting off to one side, facing a blank wall: she has been placed there because from this position she can see neither the student nor the movie screen.

The grisly film whirls on and the student squirms in her chair as the seconds flick slowly, silently by. Then at last a subtitle appears on the screen—her instructions. She is to describe the film dishonestly, as if it showed flowers, or children playing in a park. There's a rustle of clothing, the scrape of a chair being moved as the interviewer, in response to a signal, at last turns to face the student. And the girl fakes a brave smile and begins: "It must be spring. I've never seen so many pretty flowers."

This highly ingenious experiment was designed by Paul Ekman, who is young, dynamic, very outspoken and possibly the most important psychologist in the non-verbal field. His headquarters are at Langley Porter Institute in San Francisco in an old brownstone, a building with high ceilings, lots of old oak, and long wooden staircases. The atmosphere is comfortably in-formal—a staff of twenty-odd researchers dash about in shirt sleeves—but the equipment is formidable. Other scientists speak with awe of Ekman's on-line video-tape computer. He and his staff designed it themselves, and he has only to feed it a request—to ask it, for example, for all the samples in his voluminous files of hand-to-mouth gestures—and within seconds pictures materialize on a television screen. He can slow the tape down or stop it altogether for a really close look.

Ekman's interest in communication goes back to 1953, when he began looking for a way to measure what goes on in group therapy. He became convinced that what was *said* during a therapy session didn't provide any real answers, so he began to investigate nonverbal behavior. For the past seven years a fellow scientist, Wallace Friesen, has collaborated with Ekman on all his projects. Though together they have studied all types of body movements, they have concentrated especially on the face.

The purpose of the film experiment was to learn something about deception. When a person is lying, what are the tip-offs in facial expression and body motion that give him away? The student nurse was video-taped as she talked about the film. She had already had two previous sessions at the lab during which she was shown films that were quite innocuous and cheerful and she was told to describe them honestly. Now her body movements in the sessions at which she told the truth and the one in which she lied could be compared to see if in some ways she leaked the fact that she was lying.

All of the subjects recruited by Ekman for this experiment were student nurses because, as he says, "It's not a film I would want to show to anyone except someone who has to learn to deal with this kind of thing." Most of them lied passionately because they really wanted to learn not to react visibly to body mutilation. Results showed, however, that the nurses fell into three distinct categories: some were astonishingly good deceivers. A first, careful analysis of their behavior failed to turn up any clues to the fact that they were lying. Others, apparently incapable of deceiving, during the stress-film session quickly gave up and confessed. And some lied but not perfectly. One tip-off was their gestures. They did less of the casual gesticulation that normally accompanies and illustrates speech—marking time, drawing pictures in the air, pointing, sketching direction or size. Instead, more of the motions they made tended to be nervous, picky ones: lip licking, eye rubbing, scratching, and so on.

Preliminary analysis of the girls' facial expressions suggested that the clues there would turn out to be found in onset, offset, and duration. In other words, most people know how to fake a happy face or an angry or sad one, but what they don't know is how suddenly to make it appear, how long to keep it on, and how quickly to let go of it. What novelists call a "fixed smile" is an excellent example of this.

To a considerable extent, a man can control his face and use it to convey messages. It also publishes his character, since habitual expressions eventually leave their traces behind. But it is the face as conveyor of emotions that has interested psychologists. Over the years, they have been especially concerned with two questions: Does the face reliably communicate emotions? And, if so, are such facial messages sent and understood universally by all mankind? Paul Ekman, in a new book, *Emotion in the Human Face*, examines face experiments over the past half century and concludes that, reanalyzed and taken together, they prove that facial expressions *are* a reliable index to certain basic emotions. To the layman, this may seem like belaboring the obvious, but for Ekman it's an important point to prove, since much of his present work is predicated on his belief that there is a kind of vocabulary of the face.

Over a thousand different facial expressions are anatomically possible, and face muscles are so hair-trigger that theoretically a man could demonstrate all these expressions in just two hours. But only a few have a real, unequivocal meaning, and Ekman believes that those few are rarely seen full strength "except in kitchens, bedrooms and bathrooms," since etiquette requires that in most situations they be controlled. (Think of the difference between a real snarl of rage, an exaggerated teeth-baring expression seen only at moments of extreme emotion, and the slight scowl and tense mouth that are more usual.)

Ekman's problem was to find a reliable method of decoding expressions. Eventually, working with Wallace Friesen and psychologist Silvan Tomkins, he hit on an ingenious solution—a kind of atlas of the face, called Facial Affect Scoring Technique, or FAST. FAST catalogues facial expressions—using photographs instead of verbal descriptions—according to three areas: forehead and eyebrows; eyes; and the rest of the face—nose, cheeks, mouth, chin. For the emotion of "surprise," then, FAST provides photos of wrinkled foreheads above raised brows; of wide-open eyes; and of mouths opened to varying degrees in the "oh!" of astonishment. Someone wanting to categorize a facial expression can simply compare the face he's interested in, area by area, with the photographs in FAST. No verbal labels are necessary.

Ekman is now using FAST in a kind of visual-sensitivity training. The object is to teach people—salesmen, lawyers, anyone who is interested—to do better at recognizing facial expressions of emotion in everyday conversation. Ekman begins by teaching the basic expressions, then goes on to blends of emotions, where one area of the face displays one emotion while other areas display a different one (for example, angry eyes and brow above a smiling mouth). There is almost the same effect when expressions follow one another in rapid succession. Blends occur when both emotions are felt or when habit links one to another. For one man, anger may be strongly linked to fear, if his own anger frightens him; for another, fear may be linked to shame.

Ekman's trainees are also taught to distinguish between expressions that are easy to confuse, such as anger and disgust, or hurt and surprise, and to recognize emotions that have been damped down. The *pièce de résistance*, though, is the lesson in how to tell an honest expression from a dishonest one. The training uses lots of exposures, both in video-tapes and still photos. The trainees were tested afterwards on video-tapes of the deception experiment. When shown only head shots of the nurses, they could usually distinguish, just from the facial expressions, the times when the girls were lying from the times when they weren't. People with no training, shown the same shots, generally could not make these distinctions.

It seems likely that FAST will prove an invaluable tool for the psychologists who study emotion. It's hard to be sure what another human being is feeling. You can ask him, but he may refuse to answer, may lie, or may not even know what he feels. An experimenter in a lab can measure a subject's heart rate or breathing or GSR (galvanic skin response), but while these do signal the presence of emotion, they don't usually differentiate between one emotion and the next. Sometimes an experimenter looks at the situation the subject is in and guesses what emotion it would be likely to arouse, but the pitfalls are obvious.

Before FAST can be taken seriously by scientists, it must be proved reliable. One question we might ask is whether subjects trained in its use come to the same conclusions about what they see. But Ekman's experiments have shown that they do. The next question is harder to answer: Does FAST measure what people really feel? The difficulty is, as I mentioned earlier, the impossibility of knowing with any certainty what an individual is feeling, since you can't just take his word.

The question of universal expressions has preoccupied those who do face research, and over the years, Paul Ekman and Ray Birdwhistell have had a running argument about it. Ekman believes he has now proved in cross-cultural studies that there *are* universals—that men all over the world smile when they are happy or want to appear happy, and scowl when they are angry or want to look angry. As I've said, Birdwhistell maintains that certain anatomically similar expressions may occur in all men, but that the meaning people attach to them differs from culture to culture. This is, however, a minority opinion. Most scientists in the field believe that some expressions, at least, are universal.

The proof most often cited by those who believe in universals is the studies that have been done on children who were born blind. It has been found that all babies produce a social smile at the age of about five weeks, even blind babies, who couldn't be imitating the faces of those around them. Blind children also laugh, cry, pout, and wear the typical expressions of anger, fear, and sadness.

Ekman's own evidence, however, is a cross-cultural study he did with Friesen. Using carefully selected photographs of faces wearing, full strength, the primary expressions—joy, surprise, fear, anger, sadness, and disgust-or-contempt—he asked people in the United States, Brazil, Japan, New Guinea, and Borneo to identify these expressions, and most of them could, most of the time, Even the Fore succeeded, and the Fore are a Neolithic New Guinea tribe who were isolated from the modern world until just twelve years ago. At about the same time that Ekman was doing his study in South Pacific jungles and on American college campuses, another psychologist, Carroll Izard, was doing similar research in ten literate cultures and coming up with similar, affirmative results.

But Ekman doesn't advocate interpreting a Fore smile, for example, as invariably a smile of pleasure. There are what he calls "display rules" in every culture which define what expressions are appropriate in any given situation. They may call for an expression to be played down, played up, disguised, or suppressed entirely. And each culture not only has its own rules but its own facial style—Italians, whose facial behavior is volatile and highly expressive, sometimes find the facially restrained English hard to fathom.

Display rules were neatly demonstrated in an experiment Ekman recently ran in America and in Japan, where etiquette demands a smile in practically every situation. Ekman's setup was identical on both sides of the Pacific. Subjects sat alone in a room to watch a stress film, only a little less horrifying than the film the student nurses saw. While they watched it they were video-taped; they had no inkling that they were on camera. Afterwards, an interviewer entered the room, a Japanese interviewer in Japan, an American in the States, and the subject was asked to describe what he had just seen. While actually watching the film both Japanese and Americans had shown similar facial reactions, moving the same facial muscles at approximately the same points in time. During the interview, the Americans continued to react visibly, running through a whole repertoire of surprise and disgust faces, but the Japanese described what they had seen while wearing a polite smile. Only occasionally, as they looked away from the interviewer to organize their thoughts, there was just a flash of visible emotion, perhaps disgust or anger, expressions too swift to see except on film run in slow motion.

Ekman's concept of display rules and Birdwhistell's admission that, anatomically speaking, there *are* universal facial expressions appear to move the two sides of this particular debate closer together, although the points of view and the methods of research advocated by each side are very different. What is evidence to Birdwhistell is mere unproved anecdote to Ekman, while Birdwhistell believes psych-lab experiments are often contrived, artificial, and unrelated to real life.

The next logical question is: If there really are facial expressions that are universal to mankind, how did they evolve?

Charles Darwin began the inquiry in 1872 with *The Expression of the Emotions in Man and Animals*. He compared the facial expressions of a number of mammals, including man, and suggested that all the primary human expressions could be traced back to some primitive, functional act. The snarl of rage, for example, might have evolved from baring the teeth to bite.

The evolution of the smile is harder to explain, and a number of different theories have been advanced. Richard J. Andrew, for example, starts from the fact that some primates, when threatened, set up a shrill protest, a characteristic screeching produced with lips drawn back in what looks like a grin. Rhesus monkeys do this, and they sometimes put on a defensive-threat grin without bothering to make the noise. Man also uses a defensive smile, but as an appeasement gesture: think of the guest, smiling uneasily in greeting as he arrives an hour late for dinner. Weak as it is, his smile is an important buffer against aggression, for smiles supply a tenuous but vital link between men. There are wartime stories that tell how a soldier, primed for combat, who surprised an enemy was sometimes literally disarmed if the other man smiled or held out a morsel of food.

The smile of real pleasure is harder to explain than the defensive smile, but Andrew suggests that it may be a descendant of the grimacelike grin that many mammals, including man, make automatically when startled. That grin of surprise could have evolved into the broad smile of pleasure; adult humor still depends on surprise.

In 1966 two psychologists, Ernest Haggard and Kenneth Isaacs reported that, while running psychotherapy films through in slow motion, they had noticed expressions on the faces of their subjects that were on and then over with in a fraction of a second. When the film was run through at regular speed, the expressions were invisible; when it was slowed to about one-sixth normal speed, they could be picked up by most people. Further study suggested that these high-speed expressions were revealing. It seemed that very often they occurred when a patient was in conflict. "I was *not* angry," he would say while—momentarily—looking very annoyed. Often they didn't jibe with the facial expressions that bracketed them. As a patient talked about how much he really liked someone, his expression might flick from pleasure to anger and back to pleasure again. Haggard and Isaacs suggested that these expressions, which they called "micromomentary" expressions or "micros," are not intended as messages, consciously or unconsciously, but are leakage of true feelings. They may actually serve as a safety valve, permitting a person to express, very briefly, his unacceptable impulses and feelings.

Apparently, micros are not necessarily always invisible. Since the eighteen nineties numerous experiments on subliminal perception have demonstrated that we often see more than we think we do. Many people will remember the flap over subliminal persuasion in the nineteen fifties. An American market researcher claimed to have increased sales of Coke and popcorn at a movie house by repeatedly projecting the words "Eat popcorn" and "Drink Coca-Cola" on the screen while a film was being shown. The ads were flashed over and over, each time for the space of just one three-thousandth of a second—they were, in effect, invisible writing. When the experiment was made public, many Americans worried out loud about having their subconscious persuaded—the political implications were frightening. However, other experiments indicate that this is far from the most efficient form of soft sell. The boundary between the visible and the subliminal varies from one person to the next, and, for each individual, from one occasion to the next. A message flashed long enough to ensure that it would be picked up subliminally by the majority of any audience would probably be seen quite clearly and consciously by some people.

Such individual differences in perception were clearly demonstrated in an experiment Paul Ekman ran. In this, his first attempt to investigate micromomentary expressions, he showed a film that included several micros both to college students and to public health nurses. The students missed the micros completely when the film was run at normal speed but were able to catch them when it was shown in slow motion; however, the nurses, women with ten years or more of experience, spotted the micros right away during the normal-speed screening.

Going on from there, Ekman began studying micros with a tachistoscope, a machine that can flash pictures on a screen at speeds up to one one-hundredth of a second. When he fed it photographs from his stock of faces at top speed, subjects insisted they saw nothing at all.

> The T-scope experiment is my favorite magician game [Dr. Ekman said]. You run a person through it and he thinks he's looking at a blank screen. So he makes what he insists are wild guesses and then you tell him, "Now I'm going to prove to you that you got most of that right." You read him his first ten answers, and he's astounded. We have all the perceptual apparatus to decode faces at one one-hundredth of a second, which raises a very interesting question: Why don't we use it? I think we teach people systematically in childhood not to pay attention to these brief facial behaviors, because they reveal too much.

Obviously, such teaching is done on a subconscious level.

In a way, a tachistoscope is a fairly realistic way to present a face, since facial expressions are often over in just half to three-quarters of a second and are always embedded in preceding and following expressions, accompanied by a distracting stream of body movement and speech. The human eye has to be quick to see them, and so a face flashed by a tachistoscope is perhaps closer to what we're presented with in real life than is a photograph we can study at leisure.

In the course of his T-scope experiment, Dr. Ekman discovered an interesting phenomenon. About half the people he tested consistently missed on one emotion. Each of these subjects had his own particular blind spot. He might get everything else right, but he would miss almost all the photographs of faces displaying anger, for example, or disgust; it was always one of the unpleasant emotions—nobody missed on joy. Obviously there was some subconscious block at work, and it appeared to be related both to personality and to the mood of the moment.

Ekman investigated this block further in another preliminary study in which he tested thirty subjects on the T-scope, then gave them a chance to relax with a cigarette and a drink. For ten of these subjects there was a lot of alcohol in the drink; for another ten there was marijuana in the cigarette; and for the rest the drink was nonalcoholic and the cigarette was plain tobacco, a double placebo effect. When all the subjects were tested again with the T-scope, the double placebo group performed much as they had on the earlier test. The alcohol group got very slightly worse on recognizing all the emotions except disgust, and on disgust they were now much more accurate. But it was the performance of the pot group that particularly interested Ekman, since the folklore about marijuana holds that it's a great sensitivity heightener. Actually, the pot group become significantly worse at recognizing sadness and fear and slightly worse on anger. Ekman emphasizes that this was a preliminary study. What he didn't investigate was mood—marijuana and alcohol both have a way of producing quite different moods on different occasions—and so he put a more elaborate study in the works.

Most of the researchers I met who were involved in nonverbal communication studies felt that they were still doing really basic science and that practical applications of their work were a long way off. But Paul Ekman believes that nonverbal studies will be a "very hot field" for just a few more years, because that is how long it will take to answer most of the fundamental questions. As for practical applications, he forecasts a great many psychological studies of emotion, using facial expression as a measure.

There won't be any great leap forward in psychotherapy, Ekman feels, since therapists are already using the new knowledge about communication; but there will be tremendous commercial exploitation.

> I expect to see training institutes set up to train salesmen and job applicants [he said]. I expect there will be widespread monitoring of facial expressions during personnel interviews. I expect to see measurements of facial behavior used to pretest commercials—I've been approached already myself to set up all these things. No, I haven't accepted. And I expect to see business do quite explicit grooming and training of employees' facial behavior right across the board. I think it's quite possible to teach people to be better deceivers.

Some of these are uncomfortable predictions, but when I said so, Ekman's reply was that as soon as nonverbal behavior becomes part of public knowledge, it will begin to change. As soon as studies are published describing the ways in which people betray the fact that they're lying, those particular leaks will disappear, perhaps to be replaced by others. It presents an odd problem for the social scientist: his behavioral studies may eventually precipitate changes in behavior which may in turn invalidate his earlier research.

The idea of a personnel interviewer trained to "monitor" facial expressions is somewhat chilling, a reminder of George Orwell's *1984*, where a man committed a "facecrime" when his facial expression gave away the fact that he was thinking forbidden thoughts. Told body movements communicate, some people feel exposed, helpless, shown up even in silence; after all, one can refuse to speak but one can hardly refuse to move a muscle. Freud wrote, "He that has eyes to see and ears to hear may convince himself that no mortal can keep a secret. If his lips are silent, he chatters with his fingertips; betrayal oozes out of him at every pore." I once heard a man say to a woman, "Do you realize that you just crossed your legs *and* folded your arms? You're obviously feeling very defensive." Here was an intrusion upon privacy, which was as wrong as the reading and discussion of another person's mail.

Many people will be less than enchanted with the slightly ludicrous prospect of living in a world in which, as some people take lessons in reading faces, others will be learning to tell facial lies. However, this kind of tit-for-tat educational process is probably as old as mankind: one man learns to make a spear, another invents a shield, the first improves his spear, and so on.

In any case, I believe that the potential benefits of the science far outweigh the potential misuses. For, as people become more face conscious, how can they help becoming more attuned to the feelings of others? Husband and wife, patient and therapist, will be able to interpret each other better, to catch on more quickly to distress, anger, or pleasure, to assess more accurately the impression they're making on one another.

And if at the same time people become more aware of what their own faces are doing, they may end by getting into closer touch with their own feelings. And that, really, is what encounter groups, psychotherapy, the youth culture, and other modern-day phenomena are all about.

What the Eyes Tell

8

Imagine that one day, while seated in a public place, you glance up to find a stranger looking straight at you with a steady, expressionless gaze that doesn't falter even when you meet his eyes. Almost certainly, you quickly look away and then in a few seconds glance back at him to see if he's still staring. If he is, you may repeat this swift, surreptitious back-and-forth glance a number of times and as you do so, if the stare continues, you pass rapidly from discomfort to anger or alarm.

The direct, unwavering stare is a form of threat to many animals as well as to man. A naturalist who studied mountain gorillas in the wild[1] reported staring contests between males. He himself risked an attack if he watched an animal too fixedly.

[1]George Schaller in the book, *The Year of the Gorilla* (University of Chicago, 1964).

Rhesus monkeys also react violently when stared at, by another monkey or by a human. In recent laboratory experiments, Ralph Exline, a psychologist at the University of Delaware, investigated man-monkey communication in terms of eye behavior. The monkeys were housed in cages in a bare, brightly lit room. When the experimenter approached a monkey with lowered eyes and meek posture, there was minimal reaction. When the experimenter approached more aggressively, making eye contact with a deadpan stare, the animal would often bare its teeth and begin to bob its head menacingly—but the monkey would not respond as if threatened if the experimenter wore the same deadpan expression but closed his eyes. When, carrying the experiment a step further, he lunged forward and shook the cage, still with his eyes closed, even then the animal was apparently not threatened, although alerted.

Monkeys are sensitive to the stare to an almost uncanny degree. In another experiment, rhesus monkeys were stared at by a man who was hidden from them. They soon began to behave as if depressed and when their brain waves were monitored it was found that each time the man stared directly at them, there were distinct changes in the pattern of the waves. How they were able to tell whether he was looking at them or away from them, since they couldn't see him, is a mystery, but the behavior seems related to a common human experience: most of us at one time or another have had the uneasy feeling that we were being watched and then have had the suspicion confirmed when we turned around. Usually, we assume that some small sound, or a movement caught in peripheral vision, must have provided a tip-off. The idea that for monkeys, and perhaps also for men, there may be some more primitive clue is an intriguing one. Nobody knows what happens to a man's brain waves when he is stared at, but a recent study indicates that a person who is looked at a lot tends to have a higher heart rate than someone who isn't. One of the discomforts of public speaking is facing all those staring eyes.

The potency of the threatening stare has been recognized throughout human history and in many different cultures in tales of the evil eye—the gaze that can injure whatever it falls upon. There are references to a deity with an evil eye in clay tablets inscribed in the third millenium B.C. The Hebrew scholar, Rab, in the third century A.D. held that ninety-nine out of a hundred deaths were caused by it. People believed that sometimes these strange ocular powers were acquired in a pact with the devil and in other cases they were a curse visited on the innocent. Pope Pius IX, elected in 1846, was said to be an innocent possessor of the evil eye. His blessing was thought to be absolutely fatal.[2]

There has been a parallel belief in the use of large, staring eyes as defensive magic, and even as late as 1947, ships that plied the Mediterranean still often had a protective eye painted on their prows. In 1957, there was testimony before a Congressional committee about an American employer who hired a man to come in every so often and glare at his work force, a wordless threat intended to keep them hard at work.

Why the taboo on staring? It can, of course, be explained as part of the biological inheritance we share with other primates. Experiments with human infants have shown that the first sight they respond to is a pair of eyes or any configuration—such as two dots on a small, white card—that resembles eyes, and some scientists take this as evidence that the human response to eyes is innate. However, another explanation is also possible.

[2]The history of the evil eye is beautifully described in Silvan Tomkins' book *Affect, Imagery, Consciousness*, volume 2.

Where a person looks signals what he's paying attention to. When man (or a monkey) treats another to a prolonged stare, he indicates that his attention is concentrated on the other but gives no sign of what his intentions are—which is enough to make even a primate nervous. This might also explain why some people feel so uncomfortable in an encounter with a blind person. His eye behavior supplies few clues to his intentions.

Though all cultures seem to discourage staring, some are more stringent than others. One psychologist, Silvan Tomkins, has pointed out that most societies have a taboo on too much intimacy, too much sex, and a too-free expression of the emotions; what constitutes "too much" varies from culture to culture, but to the extent that these three taboos exist, there also exists a taboo on eye contact, because it heightens intimacy, expresses and simultaneously escalates emotions, and is an important element in sexual exploration.

Americans interpret prolonged eye contact as a sign of sexual attraction that they must scrupulously avoid except in appropriately intimate circumstances. It's easy for a man to signal sexual intent with the eyes: by a long direct look at breasts, buttocks, or genitals, or by a sweeping, head-to-toe undressing glance, or simply by making eye-to-eye contact. Perhaps the fact that eye contact escalates sexual excitement so rapidly accounts for that easily recognizable street-corner pattern—the man's direct challenging stare, followed quickly by the woman's lowered eyes.

Children are taught not to stare at breasts and genitals. They're seldom warned in so many words not to do it; nevertheless, they learn. In many if not all societies, the female child gets stricter where-to-look training than the male child. The connection between sex and eye contact is, in fact, a strong one. Too much sex has long been supposed to lead to eye disease and blindness.

When two people look, they share the knowledge that they are both pleased to be together, or that both are angry, or that they are both sexually aroused. We can read another person's face without meeting his eyes, but when eyes meet not only do we know how he feels, but he knows that we know. And somehow eye contact makes us feel—vividly—open and exposed and vulnerable. Perhaps that's part of the reason people so often make love in the dark, avoiding the one kind of contact—eye contact—most likely to deepen sexual intimacy.

Jean-Paul Sartre once suggested that eye contact is what makes us really, directly aware of another person as a human being with a consciousness and intentions of his own. Certainly, when eyes lock there is a special kind of human-to-human awareness. A girl who has taken part in political demonstrations reported that she was advised, if a policeman confronted her, to look straight into his eyes. If she could make him see her as another human being, she was told, he'd be more likely to treat her as one. In situations where intimacy has to be held to a minimum, for example when a butler serves a houseguest or when an officer reprimands an enlisted man, the subordinate will usually avoid eye contact by keeping his gaze directed stiffly in front of him.

The cross-cultural differences in eye behavior are considerable and sometimes important. Anthropologist Edward Hall has observed that Arabs sometimes stand very close together for conversation and look intently into one another's eyes as they talk. At the other end of the spectrum there are societies in the Far East where it is thought rude to look at the other person at all during conversation. To the American, the prolonged gaze of the Arab is anxiety-provoking, but averting the eyes completely, as is customary in the Far East, would seem a symptom of mental illness. The American even finds

British eye etiquette a bit odd, for the Englishman, except when conversing at close quarters, focuses steadily on the eyes of the other person. The Englishman also does much less nodding than the American, for it's his eyeblinks and that attentive stare that signal that he's listening. The American way is to keep constantly shifting the gaze from eye to eye or away from the face altogether.

Eye etiquette on public streets also varies from one country to the next. "My first day in Tel Aviv was disturbing," one traveler recalled. "People not only stared right at me on the street, they actually looked me up and down. I kept wondering if I was uncombed or unzipped or if I just looked too American. Finally, a friend explained that Israelis think nothing of staring at others on the street." And in France, it's quite permissible for a man to stare at a woman openly in public. In fact, some French women complain that they feel uncomfortable on American streets—as if they had suddenly become invisible.

In America, the rules are different. In public places, as Erving Goffman, a sociologist, has explained, Americans accord one another "civil inattention"; that is, we take enough visual notice of others to let them know that we know they're there, but not enough to seem curious or to intrude. On the streets this takes the special form of eyeing the other until he's about eight feet away, during which time sides of the street are apportioned by gesture, and then casting the eyes down as the other passes in "a kind of dimming of lights," as Goffman puts it. This is perhaps the slightest of rituals, yet it's one used constantly in our society.

To the American, to be stared at in a public place is an invasion of privacy, and to be caught staring is an embarrassment. Most people have encountered the where-to-look problem when sharing a small, confined space, such as an elevator, with just one other person.

On the other hand, when you're meeting someone in a public place and you've never seen him before, the taboo on staring provides an easy way to pick him out: he's the one man who violates the rule and gives you a direct and searching look. Homosexuals report that they can often spot another homosexual in a public place simply by the fact that he allows them to catch his eye. Acid heads say they spot other heads the same way.

Even films take into account the taboo on staring. One of the immediately visible differences between a home movie and a commercial film is that only in home movies do people look directly into the camera as if acknowledging the watching audience. This is a rule that has sometimes been violated most effectively. In one of the opening scenes of Fellini's *Satyricon* two beautiful young men wander through a kind of human anthill populated with beings so gross and freakish that they seem hardly human at all. The nightmare quality of the scene is enormously intensified by the fact that now and then, as the camera tracks, one of the freaks approaches and peers directly into it, thus involving the audience in an unexpected and distinctly uncomfortable way.

Most encounters begin with eye contact. As an opening gesture, it has distinct advantages—it can be so tentative that the looker need not own up and take responsibility for it, as he would have to if he spoke his greeting. Nevertheless, as Goffman has pointed out, once an American has allowed another to catch his eye, he's held to be open to whatever follows. That's why waitresses develop such skill at not allowing their eyes to be caught when they're particularly busy. Children learn this particular function of eye contact very early. When he was just two years old, my son, confined in a car seat and longing to complain, would keep turning his head to look at me but he wouldn't say a word until I allowed him to catch my eye.

Establishing eye contact or failing to establish it can

change the whole meaning of a situation. The man, running to catch a bus, who reaches it just as the door closes and the driver pulls out from the curb, eyes on the road, would feel rather differently if, as the doors closed and the bus pulled out, the driver were looking straight at him. Even etiquette makes a strong distinction between cutting a person by pretending not to see him and cutting him directly—looking at him and refusing to recognize him, a much more serious matter.

Eye behavior is perhaps the subtlest form of body language. Culture programs us in childhood, teaching us what to do with our eyes and what to expect of other people. As a result, when a man shifts his eyes and meets another person's gaze or fails to meet it, he produces an effect that's out of all proportion to the trifling muscular effort he has made. Even when each actual eye contact is fleeting, as it generally is, the sheer cumulative amount of time he spends looking at the other conveys certain things.

The movements of the eye, of course, determine what a man sees; communication research has turned up the unexpected fact that they also regulate his conversation. During the everyday exchange of words, while people focus their attention on what is being said, their eye movements provide a system of conversational traffic signals, notifying another individual when it's his turn to talk.

This discovery was made in a study done in Britain by Dr. Adam Kendon. Pairs of students, strangers to each other, were brought to his lab, asked to sit down and get acquainted, and then were filmed as they talked. Although the students varied enormously in how much time they spent looking at a companion during a conversation—the range was from twenty-eight percent to over seventy percent of the time—a very clear pattern emerged.

Imagine two people—call them John and Alison— who meet in a hallway. Preliminary greetings over, Alison begins to talk. She starts by looking right away from John; then, as she hits her conversational stride, she glances back at him from time to time, usually as she pauses at the end of a phrase or sentence. When she does, he nods his head or murmurs "uh-huh" or otherwise indicates that he's listening, and she then looks away again. Her glances at him last roughly as long as her glances away from him do, but she doesn't look at him during hesitations or speech errors. And as she comes to the end of what she wants to say, she gives him a significantly longer glance. Indications are that if she fails to do this, John, not recognizing that it's his turn to talk, will hesitate or say nothing at all.

When John takes up the conversation, Alison, listening, spends much more time looking at him than she did when she herself was the speaker. Her away glances are generally few and brief. And now when their eyes meet, it's her turn to make some reassuring sign.

It's not hard to see the logic behind this eye behavior. Alison looks away at the start of her statement and during hesitations to avoid being distracted while she organizes her thoughts. She glances at John from time to time for feedback: to make sure he's listening, to see how he's reacting, or for permission to go on talking. And while he is doing the talking, she looks at him quite a lot to show that she's paying attention, that she's polite. The importance of eye behavior as a conversational traffic signal is clearly demonstrated when both parties wear dark glasses: there are many more interruptions and long pauses than there would normally be.

In his study Ke..don also found that when a speaker asked a question, he usually looked directly at the listener, unless it was a presumptuous question or one that dealt with a subject he himself was anxious about. When the listener exclaimed over something his companion had said, he tended to look at the speaker if it was a pleased exclamation and to look away if he was expressing horror, disgust, protest—unless it was an emotion he shared with the speaker, in which case he would usually drop his eyelids instead. However, Kendon cautions that all this data applies only to a fairly formal conversation; he suspects that people in their own homes and people who know each other well may not behave the same way at all.

How long one person spent looking at the other tended to match for both students in any given pair. But a student who was paired first with one person and then with a second showed marked differences in eye behavior in the two trials. This suggests that a very sensitive, totally unverbalized agreement is somehow reached when two people talk, to keep gazing to a certain level.

It also seems to be true that in polite conversations between individuals who don't know one another, mutual looking is generally played down, probably because a lot of it would shift the focus of attention from the topic of conversation to the personal relationship between the two people. One pair of students, a man and a woman, seemed to be mutually attracted. Analysis showed that the more they smiled at one another, the less they looked. It was the woman who began to avoid eye contact and she tended to look away at the particular points when the emotional level was rising. This bit of eye behavior, then, had nothing to do with the regulatory or traffic-signal function of looking but was part of her expressive vocabulary, a way of saying, "I'm embarrassed."

Eye signals change in meaning, according to their context. There's a great difference between being on the receiving end of a prolonged look when you're doing the talking—it may actually be flattering—and being subjected to the same long gaze by someone who's talking to you. To be the listener and to be stared at is unexpected and even uncomfortable. What's more, during silence, even a companionable silence, a steady gaze is usually downright unsettling. An individual can actually express many things by his eye behavior, just by exaggerating slightly the pattern. By looking *away* a lot while listening, he indicates dissatisfaction with what the other is saying. By looking *away* more than usual while speaking, he indicates that he is uncertain about what he's saying or wishes to modify it. By looking *at* the other person while listening, he indicates agreement or simply attention. By looking *at* the other a lot while speaking, he indicates that he's interested in how the other is taking his remarks and that he's pretty sure of what he's saying.

The person doing the talking can actually try to control the behavior of his listener with eye movements: he can forestall an interruption by not looking at the other or he can prod him to make responses by glancing frequently at him.

I've mentioned earlier that the amount of looking people do varies greatly—apparently, eye behavior isn't simply a matter of sharing and using the same code. A person's eye movements are also influenced by his personality, the situation he's in, his attitudes towards those he's with, and the pecking order within the conversational group. It's also true that men and women use their eyes in significantly different ways. Most of these discoveries can be attributed to the work of psychologist Ralph Exline, who over a period of years has run dozens of experiments to investigate these and other variables and the ways they interact. His subjects, usually undergraduates, are brought into a special room and given some misleading task to do; then their eye behavior is recorded or filmed through a one-way vision mirror.

One of Exline's more intriguing findings is that looking is related to liking. When one person likes another, the chances are that he will look at him more often than is usual, with glances that last a little longer than is normal. And the other will interpret this as a sign—a polite one—that his friend is not simply absorbed in the topic of conversation but is also interested in him as a person. Of course, eye behavior isn't the only clue to liking. People also go by facial expressions, by how close the other stands, by whether he touches them or not, and by what he says. But most of us find it easier to say, "I like you," with our bodies, and particularly with our eyes, than with words.

Eye behavior can be crucial in the opening stages of a friendship, partly because eye contact is so effortlessly made. In a crowded room, even before a word has been spoken between them, two people will often engage in intricate preliminaries with their eyes: making contact, shying away, questioning, probing, choosing, or rejecting. And once conversation begins it's accompanied by continual, subtle, nonverbal negotiations, in which eye behavior plays an important part.

Just as eye movements can convey attitudes and feelings, they also express personality. Some people habitually do more looking than others. Those who are by nature affectionate do a lot of looking, as do individuals who are, as the psychologists put it, high in need-affiliation. Called the "love motive," need-affiliation is the desire to form close, warm, intimate relationships with others, a need most of us have, though to varying degrees.

It's not really a surprise to learn that affectionate, friendship-oriented people and people who like each other are more apt to look into faces and eyes. There is, in fact, a lot of folk wisdom about eye movements, and under investigation some of it turns out to be true. For example, the person who is embarrassed or upset *does* usually try to avoid meeting the eyes of others; and people *do* do less looking when asked highly personal questions than they do when asked neutral ones. Furthermore, some individuals turn quite shifty eyed when they're lying.

This last fact was neatly demonstrated in one of Exline's more ingenious experiments. His subjects were, as usual, students. They were tested in pairs, and told the purpose of the experiment was to study group decision making. Each pair was shown a series of cards and asked to guess the number of dots on each card. They had to discuss their estimates together and agree on a single answer. But in every pair one student was actually a confederate of the experimenter.

After half a dozen cards had been shown, the experimenter was always called out of the room, supposedly to take a long-distance phone call. While he was gone his stooge would manage to implicate the other student in cheating by reading the experimenter's answer sheet. Some subjects actively cheated, others were reluctant but became involved as acquiescent bystanders.

When the experimenter returned, he professed increasing skepticism about the pair's answers until finally he bluntly accused them of cheating. In the rather harrowing interview that followed, the eye behavior of the hapless subject was recorded and compared to his eye behavior at an earlier, more comfortable stage of the experiment.

Exline was not out just to test the shifty-eyes theory. He wanted to see how it related to a particular personality variable—the degree to which an individual believed in manipulating others. All subjects took a paper-and-pencil test several days before they came to the lab to take part in the actual experiment. From this questionnaire, they were scored on "Machiavellianism," or their tendency to manipulate others. And it turned out that the manipulators, as they denied cheating under interrogation, met the experimenter's eyes much more steadily than the nonmanipulators did—in fact, after the accusation they actually increased their looking, though in a pre-experiment interview all had put in about the same amount of looking time. So the amount of eye contact any particular subject went in for was affected not just by his need to conceal information but by the kind of person he was.

Another important influence on eye behavior is gender. It seems that women, at least in the laboratory situation, do more looking than men do, and once they have made eye contact, hold it for longer. There are subtler differences, too. Both men and women do more looking when with someone they like, but men increase their looking time while they're on the listening end of the conversation, and women tend to do it while they're speaking. One likely explanation for these differences seems to be that we train males and females to handle their emotions differently. Women, in general, are more comfortable about expressing their emotions, and more attuned to the emotional responses of others. Apparently, women not only place more value on the kind of information one gets through looking—information about emotions—but they also have a greater need to know, especially when with someone they like, how he or she is reacting to what they're saying; in fact, if a woman is asked to carry on a conversation with someone she can't see, she talks less than she normally does; a man, conversing with a hidden partner, actually talks more.

Another experiment Exline has done throws additional light on the tie-in between eye behavior and emotionality. Exline got each of his subjects to fill out a personality inventory that asked him, among other things, how much affection he gave to others and how much he wanted to receive. Most men apparently both gave and wanted to receive less affection than most women did. However, there was overlap—some men were more affectionate than most, and some women less affectionate than the average woman. And when Exline analyzed the visual interactions of his subjects, he found that the affectionate men exchanged mutual glances with others about as much as the average woman did, while the nonaffectionate women had a looking pattern muc.. like the average man's.

Among men and also among other animals, looking patterns often reflect status. In general, the dominant animal has more eye room. When a top monkey catches the eye of a subordinate one, the subordinate will usually narrow its eyes or look away. Some ethologists believe that the dominance structure among primates is sorted out and maintained by who can look at whom, rather than by actual aggressive acts. Whenever two monkeys lock eyes and one looks away, it's a confirmation for both of them of their places in the dominance hierarchy. It's probably true among humans, too, that the executive feels free to eye the secretary, and the secretary to gaze at the mailroom clerk, and that all three would feel that something was wrong if the who-looks-at-whom patterns were sharply reversed.

So far, we've talked entirely about eye movements, as if the eye itself were as blank as a marble. However, people apparently also respond on a subliminal level to changes within the eye, to variations in the size of the pupil. A Chicago psychologist, Eckhard Hess, is pursuing this discovery in a field of study he calls "pupillometrics." In 1965 he wrote in *Scientific American*:

> One night about five years ago I was lying in bed leafing through a book of strikingly beautiful animal photographs. My wife happened to glance over at me and remarked that the light must be bad—my pupils were

unusually large. It seemed to me that there was plenty of light coming from the bedside lamp and I said so, but she insisted that my pupils were dilated. As a psychologist who is interested in visual perception, I was puzzled by this little episode. Later, as I was trying to go to sleep, I recalled that someone had once reported a correlation between a person's pupil size and his emotional response to certain aspects of his environment. In this case it was difficult to see an emotional component. It seemed more a matter of intellectual interest, and no increase in pupil size had been reported for that.

The next morning I went to my laboratory at the University of Chicago. As soon as I got there I collected a number of pictures—all landscapes except for one semi-nude "pinup." When my assistant, James M. Polt, came in, I made him the subject of a quick experiment. I shuffled the pictures and, holding them above my eyes where I could not seem them, showed them to Polt one at a time and watched his eyes as he looked at them. When I displayed the seventh picture, I noted a distinct increase in the size of his pupils; I checked the picture, and of course it was the pinup he had been looking at. Polt and I then embarked on an investigation of the relation between pupil size and mental activity.

Hess seems to have discovered a reliable and quite measurable index to what people are thinking and feeling. In his experiments, he asks subjects to peer into a specially designed viewer while he shows them slides. As the subject looks, a movie camera films his eyes, which are reflected into the camera by a mirror inside the machine. The slides are shown in pairs, with a neutral one carefully matched for brightness to the stimulus slide that follows it, so that changes in pupil size when the second one is shown cannot be said to be due to a change in light intensity. Hess has found a whole range of pupil responses, from extreme dilation when the subject was presented with a pleasant or interesting slide to extreme constriction for one that was unpleasant. Predictably, men dilated more than women did for female pinups and women more than men for male pinups and pictures showing a mother and baby. Children at all ages from five through eighteen responded more to pictures of persons of the opposite sex than to same-sex pictures, though this involuntary sign of preference didn't always match up with the child's verbal statement as to which sex he preferred.

In further experiments homosexuals responded to male pinups rather than to female, hungry people reacted more to pictures of food than did people who had just eaten, and frightening pictures got a negative, constricting reaction unless they were so frightening that they shocked; in that case, the pupil briefly enlarged and then became small. When galvanic skin response was measured at the same time, it followed a similar pattern, and GSR is considered a reliable index to emotional reaction.

Pupil size is affected not just by sight, but also by taste and sound. When subjects were given different liquids to taste, their pupils dilated for all tastes, both pleasant and unpleasant, but they dilated more for a preferred taste. Pupils also invariably expanded at the sound of music, but a country-music fan, for example, was apt to react more to the twang of a guitar than to the opening bars of Beethoven's Ninth.

When subjects were presented with problems in mental arithmetic, the pupil size began to increase as the problem was presented, reached a maximum as the person arrived at a solution, and then began to decrease. However, the pupils didn't return to their preproblem size until after the answer had been formed into words. If the person was asked to double-check his answer, the pupil size increased again. Hess believes that pupillometrics, as he calls his studies, may thus provide a way to assess a person's decision-making ability. "Embryologically and anatomically, the eye is an extension of the brain," he writes; "it is almost as though a portion of the brain were in plain sight for the psychologist to peer at."

Do people respond to changes in pupil size during everyday encounters? There's evidence to suggest that they do. Supposedly, a magician doing card tricks can spot a card preselected by a subject because his pupils enlarge when he sees it again; and Chinese jade dealers are said to watch a buyer's pupils so that they will be able to tell when he sees something he likes well enough to pay a high price for it. But the *scientific* evidence that people do react to pupil size was provided by an experiment in which Hess showed a group of photographs to male subjects. The photos included two pictures of the same pretty girl, identical in every detail except that her pupils had been retouched—in one they had been enlarged and in the other made very small. The men's responses—as measured by changes in their own pupil size—were more than twice as strong to the picture with big pupils. However, when the subjects were questioned after the experiment, most believed the pictures were identical, though a few mentioned that one face had seemed somehow softer or prettier. None had noticed the difference in the eyes, so it seems that large pupils may be attractive to men at some subliminal level, possibly because they're the response a woman makes when she's very interested in the man she's with.

Hess has also demonstrated that women prefer pictures of men with enlarged pupils—and pictures of other women with constricted ones. Male homosexuals also prefer pictures of women with small pupils and, surprisingly, so does the "Don Juan" type of male, who may be more interested in a conquest than in a genuine response. It seems, then, that we all respond, according to our own lights, to the sexual signal in pupil size.

The practical applications of pupillometrics are obvious. In the Middle Ages women sometimes used belladonna to dilate their pupils and make themselves more attractive. In our own day researchers have already used what Hess has discovered to assess the impact of advertisements and products, to study the decision-making process, and to evaluate the effects of certain kinds of experience on interracial attitudes. Pupillometrics might someday become a way to check on progress in psychotherapy—to see, for example, whether a phobia has really been routed.

However, I doubt whether pupil-watching will be of much practical use to the average citizen, working with the naked eye. Though it seems a skill all salespeople, for example, could profitably learn, circumstances are usually against it—in fact, those Chinese jade dealers must be pretty far-sighted. Aside from the risks one always runs by staring at a stranger, there is the fact that the salesman who actually succeeds in getting close enough—and in a strong light—for a good look at his customer's pupils is likely to so alarm him that the potential buyer will scuttle for cover.

For the layman, there is almost too much information available on eye behavior. What it all amounts to is one exasperating question: How on earth can any one sort out, in any given situation, what an individual is expressing by his eye movements, when they can be attributed to so many different factors? If a new acquaintance looks at you a lot, do you assume that he likes you, that he's just naturally affectionate, or that if you could test him for need-affiliation, he'd turn out to be high in love-motive? Is he so high-status that he automatically assumes he has more eye room? If this is a man-to-man confrontation, he is asserting that status? Or if you're a woman and he's a man, is this a sexual come-on? Or a put-down? These questions, in general, though they may be relevant to the scientist trying to sort out the body code, are a waste of breath for the layman. In most situations, intuition puts together many different nonverbal messages and presents you with a conclusion. Or at least an inkling.

But when that's done, it's likely that the clue you'll be most *aware* of, after facial expression, is eye behavior.

All of which brings us back to one basic but seldom noted fact: The statement "We look in order to see" is a truism which is only partly true of face-to-face encounters.

The Dance of the Hands

9

It's a tired old joke that "so-and-so would be left speechless if you tied his hands," but it's true that most of us would actually be pretty uncomfortable if we were forced to forgo the little hand dance with which we so often accompany and illustrate our words.

Most people are quite aware of the hand-dancing of others but in general they ignore it, assuming that it's just so much meaningless motion. But gestures do communicate. Sometimes they help to clarify, when the verbal message is unclear. At other times, they can unintentionally reveal emotions. Tightly clasped hands or hands that fidget are clues to tension that other people are apt to pick up. Sometimes, too, a gesture is so clearly functional that the exact meaning is unmistakable. In one research film, a woman covered her eyes whenever she spoke of something she was ashamed of, and when discussing her relationship with her therapist, she would hitch up her skirt.

Some of the most common gesticulations are actually tied to speech, as ways to illustrate or emphasize what is said. There are gestures that point to things and those that suggest distances ("He came *that* close . . .") or directions ("We have to move *forward!*"). Some depict a body action (fist-waving or juggling) and some sketch size or shape in the air. Still others time out the stages of the narrative in progress ("*Then* he sat down and *then* he said . . . ").

Every individual has his own gestural style, and in part, a person's style reflects his culture. In America, gestures are often a tip-off to ethnic origins, since every culture produces its own distinctive style of body movement and that style is actually more persistent than a dialect or "foreign" accent. Experts believe that in the United States ethnic gesture styles often last well into the third generation: for example, members of a family from southern Italy that has been in the United States for three generations may still move with the expansiveness and dramatic flair of Italians. Theoretically, a movement style could persist forever if in each generation the children were raised within the ethnic enclave. On the other hand, a child brought up in suburbia and perhaps sent away to school at an early age is likely to learn a different way of moving.

Albert Scheflen has suggested that movement style is sometimes mistaken for physical features. Perhaps when we say that someone looks French, or looks Jewish, what we mean is that he moves elegantly, like a Frenchman, or in staccato fashion, like a Jew. There are people who are bilingual and switch gesture styles when they switch languages, as Fiorello LaGuardia did.[1] Many others don't, so that we may meet someone who speaks good

[1]See p. 26.

English but with absolutely perfect Yiddish kinesics, and somehow he doesn't *sound* as if his English is as good as it is because his movements don't match it.

Gestural styles were investigated back in the early nineteen forties in a truly remarkable study by a man named David Efron. Efron wanted to refute the claims of Nazi scientists that differences in gestures were racially inherited, so he studied Jewish and Italian immigrants on New York's Lower East Side. It's hard to know whether the book that grew out of his research actually started the present wave of interest in nonverbal communication or whether scientists simply rediscovered it in the fifties, when communication research finally began in earnest.[2] But in any case Efron's *Gesture and Environment* is a mine of information on the history of gesticulation and may well be, besides, as one researcher put it, "the single most comprehensive work in kinesics." Efron used a variety of research techniques in his study: his own observations, an artist's on-the-spot sketches, and films. To analyze the films, he drew a grid on his movie screen and made direct measurements of the pathways of gesticulations.

What he found, to begin with, was that there *were* actually considerable differences in gestural style. Jews, when they gesticulated, kept their hands fairly close to the chest and face. Their upper arms were often held close against the sides of their bodies, so that movement began at the elbow. And their gestures were mostly one-handed: choppy, staccato, and full of nervous energy. Two people talking together would often gesticulate simultaneously, and the speaker might move in close and

[2]Efron himself dropped out of sight after *Gesture and Environment* was published in 1941, and communication researchers used to speculate about what might have happened to him. Paul Ekman recently traced him to Geneva, where he had spent twenty-two years on the staff of the International Labor Organization. His book was republished in 1972.

actually seize the other by his lapels. Jews, also, were apt to use the illustrator gestures for marking time and suggesting direction. The Italian immigrants, in contrast, used more of the acting-out and sketching-out gestures, which tended to be expansive, sweeping, two-handed, symmetrical. Their hands moved in all directions, sometimes flowing out to arm's length. The Italians were also more apt to touch their own bodies than those of their listeners and their movements were spirited and forceful but also smooth and even.

Efron went on to study first-generation Italians and Jews and found that those who maintained the traditional ties to the ethnic community retained its gestural style, while those who became assimilated into American life began to lose it. Efron even turned up hybrid gestures that partook a little of both the different styles. He unquestionably proved his point—that gestural styles are not racially inherited.

In 1942, in a review of Efron's study, Gardner Murphy speculated on the forces that shape the gestural style of a culture. Elaborating on explanations suggested by Efron, he wrote:

> The Italian gesture appears as the expression of a village existence where space is free, family status clearcut, and conversation much like song or dance in its expressive value. Under conditions of economic and social persecution, the European Jewish gesture tends to be a gesture of escape, or, in a struggle to cope with difficulty, a gesture of localized aggression directed to the only immediately available object. Metropolitan life in an American city makes both types of gesture less meaningful and more and more useless. It is not just the imitation of the American norm; it is the positive role of gesture in social living that requires emphasis.[3]

[3]From a 1942 book review by Gardner Murphy, published in *The Annals of the American Academy*, vol. 220.

In *Nonverbal Communication*,[4] another of the major, early books in the field, Jurgen Ruesch and Weldon Kees reviewed Efron's study and went on to describe the gesture styles of the French, Germans, and Americans.

The French, they wrote, use movements sparingly but with elegance and precision in stylized expressions of emotions. They are neither as expansive as the Italians, as insistent as the Jews, as angular and incisive as the Germans, nor as casual as the Americans. Among the Germans, the most expressive areas are the face and "the region of the spine"—referring to a characteristic, soldierlike posture—while movements of the hand and arm are generally used to reinforce statements about belief. In America, in general, gestures lack the ardent stylization of the French or the interpersonal involvements conveyed through Italian gesticulations. Moreover, there are great differences in style between regions.

Margaret Mead in *Male and Female*[5] noted those differences. Comparing the United States to simpler, less technically advanced, and consequently more homogeneous societies, where there is a single movement style for everyone, she wrote of Americans:

> All men do not cross their legs with the same assured masculinity. . . . All women do not walk with little mincing steps, or sit and lie with thighs drawn close together, even in sleep. The behavior of each American is itself a composite, an imperfectly realized version, of the behavior of others who in turn had, not a single model . . . but a hundred models, each different, each an individually developed style, lacking the authenticity, the precision, of a group style. The hand held out in greeting, to still a tear, or to help up a strange child that has stumbled, is not sure

[4]*Nonverbal Communication* by Jurgen Ruesch and Weldon Kees, University of California Press, 1956.
[5]*Male and Female; A Study of the Sexes in a Changing World.* By Margaret Mead, published by Dell, 1949.

that it will be taken, or if taken, taken in the sense in which it is offered. . . .

The speech, the gesture of Americans, include the tentativeness, the possibility of being misunderstood whenever relations go deep, the possibility of building a quick code that for the moment will do roughly, the need to feel out the other person, to find some slight, over-explicit, imperfect, immediate communication.

Just as every culture has its own distinctive movement style, each has its repertoire of emblems. An emblem is a body motion that has an agreed-upon meaning, such as the hitchhiker's thumbing or the throat-cut gesture.

Paul Ekman, in work that parallels his search for universal facial expressions, has been conducting a search for the emblems that are universal to mankind. Working in Japan, Argentina, and among the South Fore tribe in New Guinea, he has so far turned up ten to twenty emblems that are possibly universal—that is, the same body movement carries the same message in all three of these highly divergent cultures. It may not be true that every society has these emblems, but Ekman considers it probable that if a culture *does* have any emblems at all for these words or phrases, they will be the ones he has turned up in his research.

One example is sleep, indicated by inclined head, and cheek cradled on hand. Another is the emblem for being full, which involves putting the hand on the belly and either patting or rubbing it. Ekman believes it is the limitations of human anatomy that make these universal. When the musculature allows an action to be performed in more than one way, there are cultural differences in its emblem. For example, though the emblem for eating always involves a hand-to-mouth pantomime, in Japan one hand cups an imaginary bowl at about chin level while the other scoops imaginary food into the mouth;

but in New Guinea, where people eat sitting on the floor, the hand shoots out to arm's length, picks up an imaginary tidbit, and carries it to the mouth. The emblem for suicide in Argentina is to make the hand into a pistol shape and point it at the head; in Japan, it's a gut-skewering pantomime of hari-kari.

Sometimes different cultures use the same emblem but give it quite different meanings. Sticking out the tongue is a child's rude gesture in this country, but in modern south China a quick flick of the tongue signifies embarrassment; in Tibet it's a sign of polite deference; and the Marquesans stick out their tongues to say no.

Obviously, a man visiting a foreign country who uses the wrong emblem can find himself with unexpected problems. An American lecturer in Colombia, for example, was talking to his students about preschool children; but when he held his arm out, palm down, to indicate the height of the children, his class laughed. It seems that that particular gesture is used in Colombia to demonstrate the size of animals but never the size of humans. It was this kind of incident that inspired two young Fulbright scholars in Colombia to write what is probably the first teaching manual to translate emblems.[6] Though some language teachers have pointed out that people don't expect foreigners to be gesture perfect, no matter how fluently bilingual they otherwise are, it seems logical for students to learn at least a smattering of the kinesics of a language while they're absorbing its vocabulary; and it's likely that languages will be taught that way in the future.

Gesticulation has been studied from quite a different point of view by the kinesicists, who see it as one highly

---

[6]The book is *Handbook of Gestures: Colombia and the United States,* by Robert Saitz and Edward Cervenka, published by Mouton, in press.

patterned element in the surprisingly regular, even repetitious stream of body movements.

Adam Kendon has done a detailed analysis of the gesticulations of a man filmed while he was addressing an informal gathering of about eleven people. With the help of a linguist, Kendon first broke down the man's speech not into grammatical units but into phonetic ones, based on the rhythms and intonation patterns of the speech itself. He found that this two-minute talk could be analyzed into three "paragraphs," containing between them eleven "subparagraphs," which in turn were made up of eighteen locutions (each roughly the equivalent of a sentence), which could be subdivided again into forty-eight phrases.

What Kendon discovered next was rather an amazing thing. Each level of speech was accompanied by a contrasting pattern of body motion, so that when the speaker passed from one phrase to the next, or one sentence to the next, he also changed from one sort of body movement to another. During the first of the three paragraphs, for example, the man gesticulated only with his right arm; during the second, with his left; and during the third with both arms. Within a subparagraph he might use broad in-and-out movements of the whole arm during the first sentence, movements only of the wrist and fingers during the second, and then might flex his arm from the elbow during the third. The same sort of thing happened at the phrase level.

Kendon told me that the man in the film was in a sense enacting the grammatical structure of what he was saying when he gesticulated. In addition, he regularly associated particular movements with particular phrases or ideas. At one point he said, "The British are self-conscious"—holding his hands in his lap, fingers overlapping with palms facing in and thumbs up. In the next paragraph he came back to the same idea, expressing it slightly differently, but he accompanied it with the same hand position.

All this ties in rather neatly with kinesics findings on posture—that in any encounter a man arranges his body in a series of different postures; that he will have one set for speaking and another for listening and that he will even differentiate sometimes between the speaking postures, assuming one body attitude while asking questions, another when giving orders, a third for explaining, and so on. And from microanalysis it has also been reported that all a man's body motions change directions at times that coincide with the rhythms of his speech, so that even right down to the syllable level his body may dance to his spoken rhythm.

One problem that interests Kendon now is the contexts in which people do or do not gesticulate. The man in the film, he noted, was making a little speech that was probably pretty well thought out in advance and was run through rather smoothly. Knowing more or less what he was going to say next, he naturally and easily—if unintentionally—patterned his gestures to the flow of his words.

But gesticulation also occurs during hesitant speech. Kendon has observed that often, while a person pauses in mid-sentence to search for his next words, he will act them out with a hand gesture. A woman who said, "They wheeled a big table in with a-a-a big cake on it," made a horizontal, circular motion in the shape of a cake in mid-air with one finger as she hesitated on the "a-a." Kendon suggests that sometimes people may sketch with gestures what they're about to put into words. He continued:

> It's also true that if you ask somebody to repeat something because you didn't quite understand it, then if he didn't put in gesticulations before they will come out in

the repeat. They seem to appear when a person has to do more work to produce what he has to say, or where the effort he has to put into getting across to somebody is greater. It's as if the more his level of arousal is raised, the more of his body he recruits, so that you get more and more of these gesticulations.

There's support for this explanation in an experiment done by Howard Rosenfeld, a psychologist. He found that subjects who were instructed to try to make another person like them both smiled more and gesticulated more than subjects told not to be too friendly.

When a man gestures, he's only peripherally aware that he's doing it. He's slightly more aware of the hand dance of another person, but in general he looks mostly at faces rather than at hands.

Yet the hands are marvelously articulate. Seven hundred thousand different hand signals are possible, using combinations of postures, and arm, wrist, and finger movements. Edward A. Adams, an associate professor of art at Pennsylvania State University, has noted that, "Hand gestures are also economical, rapid to use, and can be executed more quickly than articulated speech."

Throughout history there have been sign languages in which gestures actually replaced speech. In fact, some scientists have suggested that man's earliest language may have been a gestural one. They point to the fact that people seem to learn sign language quite readily. Deaf-mute children will quickly invent their own system of gestural communication if they're not taught an established one.

Nevertheless, today we talk with our tongues rather than with our hands—obviously the more efficient way to do it. The human voice is capable of many rich and subtle nuances, and the man who chatters with his hands must necessarily remain speechless whenever his hands must be used in another way. Still, gesticulations do convey a great deal. They're a clue to a man's tensions, they may hint at his ethnic origins, and they're also a direct expression of his personal style.

10 | The Messages in Distance and Location

A man's sense of self isn't bounded by his skin; he walks around inside a kind of private bubble, which represents the amount of airspace he feels he must have between himself and other people. This is a truth anyone can easily demonstrate by moving in gradually on another person. At some point the other will begin, irritably or just absent-mindedly, to back away. Cameras have recorded the tremors and minute eye movements that betray the moment when the bubble is breached. It was Edward Hall, a professor of anthropology at Northwestern University, who first commented on these strong feelings about personal space, and from his work a new field of study has developed—proxemics—which he has defined as "the study of how man unconsciously structures microspace."[1]

[1]Hall developed the concept of proxemics in detail in two highly readable books, *The Silent Language*, published by Fawcett, 1959, and *The Hidden Dimension*, published by Doubleday, 1959 and 1966.

Professor Hall's particular concern is the misunderstandings that can develop because people from different cultures handle space in very different ways. For two unacquainted adult male North Americans, for example, the comfortable distance to stand for conversation is about two feet apart. The South American likes to stand much closer, which creates problems when a South American and a North American meet face to face. The South American who moves in to what is to him a proper talking distance may be considered "pushy" by the North American; and the North American may seem standoffish to the South American when he backs off to create the size gap that seems right to him. Hall once watched a conversation between a Latin and a North American that began at one end of a forty-foot hall and eventually wound up at the other end, the pair progressing by "an almost continual series of small backward steps on the part of the North American . . . and an equal closing of the gap by the Latin American."

If Americans and Latins have misunderstandings about maintaining a sociable distance, Americans and Arabs are even less compatible in their space habits. Arabs thrive on close contact. Hall has explained that "The Mediterranean Arabs belong to a touch culture and in conversation they literally envelop the other person. They hold his hand, look into his eye, and they bathe him in their breath. I once asked an Arab how he knew that he was getting through to another person . . . and he looked at me as if I was crazy and said, 'If I am not getting through to him he is dead.'"

Dr. Hall's interest in man's use of space developed in the early nineteen fifties when he was Director of the Point Four training program at the Foreign Service Institute. In talking with Americans who had lived overseas, he found that many of them had been highly distressed by cultural differences so subtle and so basic that their effects were felt for the most part at a preconscious level. Such distress is usually referred to as culture shock.

The problem is that, relatively speaking Americans live in a noncontact culture. Partly, this is a product of our puritan heritage. Dr. Hall points out that we spend years teaching our children not to crowd in and lean on us. We equate physical closeness with sex, so that when we see two people standing close together we assume that they must be either courting or conspiring. And in situations where we ourselves are forced to stand very close to another person—on a crowded subway, for example—we're careful to compensate. We avert our eyes, turn away, and if actual body contact is involved, tense the muscles on the contact side. Most of us feel very strongly that this is the only proper way to behave.

"I can't stand that guy," a stockbroker once complained about a colleague. "I have to ride down with him in the elevator sometimes and he just lets himself go. It's like being leaned on by a mountain of warm jelly."

Animals also react to space, and in ways that are predictable for each species. For example, many have both a flight distance and a critical distance. If any creature sufficiently threatening comes within flight distance of the animal, it will run; but if the animal is cornered and the menace continues to advance until within critical distance, the animal will attack. A lion tamer apparently manipulates a lion by knowing to a hair what the beast's critical distance is. The trainer steps across this sensitive boundary and the lion springs at him, landing—just incidentally—on the stool that stands between them. Instantly, the man backs off until he's beyond critical distance. And the animal stays where it is, no longer impelled to attack.

A human's personal-space bubble represents the same kind of margin of safety. Let a stranger breach the bubble and the need to flee or to strike out usually surfaces immediately. One police textbook recognized this when it advised the detective, while questioning the suspect, to sit quite close to him with no table or other obstruction between and to move even closer as the interrogation progressed.

But the degree of closeness can convey messages far subtler than a threat. Hall has suggested that it neatly expresses the nature of any encounter. In fact, he has hypothesized a whole scale of distances, each felt to be appropriate in this country for a particular kind of relationship. Contact to eighteen inches apart is the distance for wrestling or lovemaking or for intimate talk—here, even a discussion of the weather becomes highly charged. At this range people communicate not only by words but by touch, smell, body heat; each is aware of how fast the other is breathing, of changes in the pallor or texture of the skin. One and a half to two and a half feet is the close phase of what Hall calls personal distance. It approximates the size of the personal-space bubble in a noncontact culture such as ours. A wife can comfortably stand inside her husband's bubble, but she may feel uneasy if another woman tries it. Personal distance, far phase—two and a half to four feet—is still, for most people, within arm's length—the limit of physical domination. It's appropriate for discussing personal matters.

Four to seven feet is close social distance. In an office, people who work together normally stand this far apart to talk. However, when a man stands four to seven feet from where his secretary is sitting and looks down at her, it has a domineering effect. Far-phase social distance, seven to twelve feet, goes with formal conversation, and desks of important people are usually big enough to hold visitors to this distance. Above twelve feet one gets into public distances, appropriate for speechmaking and for very formal, stiff styles of speaking. Choosing the right distance can be crucial. A young woman I know, proposed to by a man she thought she was in love with, turned him down on the spur of the minute. What decided her was the fact that he did his proposing while sitting in a chair eight feet away.

Hall believes that human beings not only have strong feelings about space, but a real, biological need for enough elbow room. Just how important this might be is suggested by population studies done on animals. Until recently, scientists believed it was the combination of natural predators and a limited food supply that kept animal populations down in the wild. Hence, they predicted that if man overpopulated the globe, a worldwide famine and wars over food supplies would soon pare down his numbers. But now there are suggestions that space may be as crucial a need for man as food. In experiments with rats it has been observed that long before a real food problem can develop, rats become so stressed by overcrowding that they begin to behave in bizarre, unratlike—in fact, depressingly human—ways. The male rats may turn homosexual, run in packs, rape, murder, and pillage. Or they may simply drop out, becoming totally passive. The whole dismaying phenomenon is called a "behavioral sink."

For a world facing human overpopulation, the implications are alarming, though some scientists still question whether, in this case, one can or should generalize from animals to humans. There have also been suggestions that for men—and possibly rats, too—what is important isn't the amount of space available or the preservation of the personal-space bubble, but the number of others with whom the individual is forced to interact. If this is true, then, in our big cities if we can just manage to file people away neatly enough, so that not too many others impinge on them, they should survive nicely, no matter what the population density per square foot. There is also growing evidence that in some areas of the world famine may be only a few decades off —and so probably more imminent than a behavioral sink.

But in other, less dramatic ways, crowding definitely influences behavior, and it influences men and women differently. Men, crowded together in a small room, become suspicious and combative. Women in the same situation become friendlier and more intimate with one another; they're apt to like each other better and to find the whole experience more pleasant than they would if the group were convened in a larger room. In a small, crowded room an all-male jury gives a tougher verdict; an all-female jury a more lenient one.

Other psychologists have been designing experiments based on Hall's observations of American proxemic behavior, and their evidence suggests that the way humans space themselves may be determined not only by their culture and the particular relationships involved, but by other factors as well. At a crowded cocktail party, people necessarily stand closer together to talk, and experiments indicate that they also stand closer in a public place, such as a park or on the street. Adam Kendon suggests that in public people need to emphasize more strongly the fact that they're together—that they're a "with," to use the technical term—and so can lay claim to a certain small bubble of privacy. When two individuals stand closer together than their situation and the setting seem to warrant, it may be simply because they like each other. Psychological studies have shown that people choose to stand closer to someone they like than to someone they don't; that friends stand closer than acquaintances do, and acquaintances closer together than strangers. The evidence also indicates that in intimate situations introverts maintain slightly greater distances than extroverts, and that pairs of women stand closer to talk than do pairs of men.

Dr. Augustus F. Kinzel, a New York psychiatrist, has studied what he calls the "body-buffer zone" in violent and nonviolent convicts. Placing each prisoner in turn in the center of a small, bare room, Kinzel walked slowly toward him, instructing the man to speak up when he got too close. Prisoners with a record of violence reacted sharply while Kinzel was still a good three feet away, but the nonviolents didn't speak until the distance was one and a half feet. The violent men reported a feeling that he was "looming" or "rushing" at them. This experiment suggests that proxemics might someday provide a simple technique for spotting the potentially violent, but Kinzel cautions that his method apparently wouldn't single out *all* violent subjects; some have only an average-size buffer zone. "There may be other types of behavior also associated with large body-buffer zones that we don't know about yet," he points out.

Another, rather chilling series of experiments by a psychologist named Robert Kleck indicates that people who are disabled may have good reason to feel lonely or isolated because of the amount of distance from them assumed by those with whom they are in contact. Kleck asked college students to enter a room and start up a conversation with the person inside it. Sometimes he described the person as an epileptic, sometimes he didn't; the students sat farther away when told he was epileptic. When Kleck ran the same experiment using a fake amputee, he got the same results. This becomes all the more disturbing when you realize that the subject probably revealed his negative reaction in other non-verbal ways as well.

Spacing can also provide telltale status signals. People shown short, silent films of one "executive" walking into another "executive's" office were remarkably consistent in judging just how important each man was. The clues they used were time and distance ones: how long the man at the desk waited before responding to the knock on his door, how long he took to get to his feet, and how far into the room the visitor came. The farther in he ventured, the more important he was judged to be. And of course estimates of his status went down when the man behind the desk delayed in responding to him. In these small ways, hundreds of times a day, an individual silently asserts his superior status, or challenges others, or reassures them that he knows his place.

Public spatial behavior has been the subject for investigations by Robert Sommer of the University of California at Davis, and by a number of other psychologists. In one experiment done in the study hall of a college library, the researcher would pick out a victim surrounded by empty chairs and sit down in the next seat. This violated unwritten social rules, because when there was a lot of space available one was expected to keep one's distance. The victim usually reacted with defensive gestures and uneasy shifts of posture, or he edged away. And if the experimenter not only sat down in the next chair but then proceeded to hitch it closer, the victim often fled. Rarely did anyone make any kind of verbal protest, for though people have strong feelings about the proper spacing in public places, these feelings rarely find their way into words.

Americans have other unverbalized rules about space. When two or more people are talking together in public, they assume that the ground they're standing on is, temporarily, their own joint territory and that others won't intrude. Kinesicists have observed that this usually does happen. In fact, anyone who has to skirt the edges of such a conversational grouping will markedly lower his head as he does so. If the group is actually blocking his way and he has to pass through it, he adds a verbal apology to the lowered head. On the other hand, Hall has noted that, to the Arab, public space is public space. If he's waiting for a friend in a hotel lobby and another person has a better vantage point, the Arab may come and stand right next to him, moving in quite close. Very often this tactic succeeds in driving the other away— furious but silent. Unless, of course, he's also an Arab.

People sometimes try to stake out a claim to a chunk of public territory just by the location they select. In an uncrowded library, someone who simply wants to sit by himself will pick an end chair, one at the head or foot of a rectangular table; but someone who wants actively to discourage others from joining him will sit along the side in a middle chair. One can see the same kind of thing happening on park benches. If the first person to come along sits at one end of the bench, the second will sit at the other end, and after that passersby usually hesitate to take the middle position. On the other hand, assuming the bench is a short one, if the first person places himself in its exact center he may succeed in keeping it to himself for a time.

The relative position an individual chooses can be a status signal. A group leader, for example, automatically gravitates to an end chair at a rectangular table. And it seems that the average jury, meeting to pick a foreman and seated around a rectangular table, is most apt to elect one of the two individuals who occupy end chairs; furthermore, the individuals who choose to sit in those chairs in the first place are generally people with a lot of social status, who proceed to take leading roles in the discussion.

Adam Kendon points out that any group of people, when standing and talking, assumes what he calls a configuration. If the shape is circular, it's a safe bet that everyone in the group is on a more or less equal footing. Noncircles tend to have a "head" position and the person in it is usually, formally or informally, the leader. Seating arrangements are almost always physically imposed in a classroom and they can affect behavior. In a seminar if students sit in a horseshoe shape, those at the sides participate less than those at the end, who can more easily make eye contact with the instructor. When the students sit in rows, those in the center have more to say than do those at the sides and, again, easy eye contact seems to be the explanation.

Other studies have shown that when two people expect to compete they will usually sit opposite one another; expecting to cooperate, they sit side by side, while for ordinary conversation, they sit at right angles. When negotiators from two corporations hold a meeting, the teams may automatically line up facing one another across the conference table. However, if the meeting is adjourned for lunch, the men are likely to sit in alternating chairs at the restaurant tables, each negotiator sandwiched between two men from the other corporation. Once the occasion is defined as a social one, individuals are as careful to mix as they were earlier not to mix.

Space communicates. When a number of people cluster together in a conversational knot—at a party, for example, or outdoors on a college campus—each individual expresses his position in the group by where he stands. By choosing a distance, he signals how intimate he wants to be; by choosing a location, such as the head spot, he can signal what kind of role he hopes to play. When the group settles into a particular configuration, when all the shifting around stops, it's a sign that nonverbal negotiations are over. All concerned have arrived at a general, if temporary, agreement on the pecking order and the level of intimacy that's to be maintained, and perhaps on other relationships as well.

11 | Interpreting Postures

Most of us think of posture as a dull subject Mother used to harp on. But to psychoanalysts a patient's posture sometimes offers a first-class clue to the nature of his problems; and recently students of human communication have examined posture for what it expresses about a man's attitudes—about his feelings for the people he's with.

Posture is the easiest of the nonverbal clues to pick up, and becoming a posture watcher can be great fun. The first thing to watch for is the postural echo.

It was Albert Scheflen who discovered that, surprisingly often, people echo one another's body attitudes. Two friends will sit in precisely the same way, right leg crossed over left, for example, and hands clasped behind head; or else in the mirror-imaged way, one of them reversing to left leg over right. Scheflen calls these congruent postures. He believes that whenever people strongly share a point of view, they're apt to share a posture as well.

When four or more people get together, it's common for several distinct postural sets to develop. You can see very quickly that this is not just coincidence—if one person rearranges his body the other members of his set will often follow suit, until all are congruent again. And if you listen to what is being said, you usually find that those who think alike on the subject in question sit alike.

Television talk shows provide copious examples of posture matching, as does almost any party. Watching posture during an argument—live or on TV—is especially interesting, because you can sometimes see who's siding with whom even before everybody has had his say; and when a man is about to change sides, he'll often telegraph the switch by rearranging his body. However, if old friends argue they may actually take up congruent postures for the duration of the debate, as if to underline the fact of their unchanging friendship. Lovers, even in mid-quarrel, sometimes look as alike as matching book-ends. Congruence is also sometimes related to status. People who are on roughly the same level will often share a posture, but professor and student, executive and secretary, very seldom do. When an argument breaks out in a group with a leader, the leader may cross his legs to be congruent with one faction and fold his arms like the other—by doing this he refuses to take sides.

Some psychotherapists are very much aware of the implications of the postural echo. The late Frieda Fromm-Reichmann would sometimes assume a patient's posture to try to get a better idea of what he was feeling. Other therapists use congruence in a different way. One researcher, who analyzed a psychotherapy film for the relationship between posture matching and moments of verbal rapport, discovered only afterward that the therapist had deliberately echoed his patient's postures as a way to *promote* rapport.

Just as congruent postures express rapport, noncongruent postures can be used to establish psychological distance. There is a film made in a women's dormitory that shows a young couple side by side on a sofa; the girl is turned toward the man, who sits facing outward, with arms and legs arranged as if to put a barrier between himself and her. For eight minutes he sits stolidly so, from time to time turning just his head toward the girl as he talks to her. At the end of that time another young woman enters and the man gets up and goes off with her—by his posture he had been establishing the fact that the girl he was sitting with was not his date.

Sometimes, when people are forced to sit closer together than is comfortable, they unconsciously deploy their arms and legs as barriers. Two men, squeezed together side by side on a sofa, will turn slightly aside and cross their legs from the inner side out, or they may put up a hand or arm to shield their faces on that mutual side. A man and woman seated facing each other at close quarters will cross their arms and perhaps their legs and lean back in their chairs. People also use their bodies to establish boundaries. When friends stand or sit in a line, the individuals at each end will often extend an arm or a leg as if to exclude outsiders.

Shifts of posture appear to parallel spoken language, just as gesticulations sometimes do. Scheflen found that during conversation an individual shifts his head and eyes every few sentences, usually just as he has finished making a point, and makes a major shift of his whole body to coincide with a change in point of view—from that of listener to that of speaker, for example. Even during sleep postural shifts occur at logical end points. Sleep scientists report that people move around in bed between dreams or between episodes in a dream but seldom during the dream action itself.

Scheflen also found that most people work from postural repertoires that are surprisingly limited, and produce their shifts in predictable sequences. In one film he worked on, the patient turned his head to the right and avoided the woman therapist's eyes whenever she spoke; looked directly and challengingly at her each time he answered; and then, usually, as he went off on a conversational tangent, would cock his head and turn his eyes to the left.

Every individual has a characteristic way of holding his body when he sits, stands, and walks. It's something as personal as his signature, and often it appears to be a reliable clue to his character. Think of the difference between the way John Wayne moves—straight, solid, unbending—and the loose, slightly stooped stance of another tall man, Elliott Gould. Most of us can recognize the people we know well, even when they're still a long distance off, by the way they walk or sometimes just by the way they stand.

A man's posture recalls his past. The very set of his shoulders can hint at burdens borne, or rage held back, or a habit of timidity. At centers such as the Esalen Institute it is believed that sometimes personal psychological problems become embedded in the body structure. A woman goes through a long period of depression and her body slumps, her shoulders become stooped under the weight of her problems. Perhaps the cause of her depression disappears, but the posture remains, since some muscles have shortened, others have stretched, and new connective tissue has formed. Because her body still sags with depression, she may continue to feel depressed. It's possible, though, that if her body could be retrained, put back into proper balance, her psyche would benefit. These theories are part of somatopsychic medicine, which assumes that the state of the body affects the state of the emotions. (Psychosomatic medicine, on the other hand, assumes that emotions affect body.) Alexander

Lowen, a psychiatrist, combines psychotherapy with physical therapy. Another technique—called Rolfing for its inventor, Ida Rolf—involves strenuous, painful massage aimed at releasing and re-positioning chronically tense, contracted muscles. Although Rolfing doesn't try to build insight, it sometimes descends, overwhelmingly, on patients while they're being Rolfed.

Posture is not only a clue to character, it's also an expression of attitude. In fact, many of the psychological studies that have been done on posture analyze it for what it reveals about the individual's feelings about the people he's with.

During the trial of the Chicago Seven, their defense attorney, William Kunstler, made a formal objection to the judge's posture. He pointed out that during the prosecution's summation Judge Julius Hoffman leaned forward, all attention, but during the summation by the defense he leaned so far back in his chair that he seemed almost asleep. The objection was overruled.

For many social situations in our culture, there are postures that are considered proper and improper. One doesn't lie down during a business meeting or prop one's feet on the table at dinner. And one can, quite deliberately, convey a message by assuming a posture inappropriate to the situation.

Among Americans, posture can be a tip-off not only to relative status but to whether two people like one another or not; and the signals are slightly different for men and for women. It has been observed by one experimenter that when a man is leaning forward slightly but is relaxed with his back a little curved, he probably likes the person he's with. On the other hand, if he lounges far back in his chair, it may be a sign of dislike. However, if he's with another man and both dislikes him and feels threatened by him—the mail clerk getting instructions from the vice-president, for example—he may instead sit up very straight and tense. But if he's with a *woman* he dislikes, he always signals it only by lounging back; apparently, no woman is threatening enough to make any man sit tensely at attention. Women show liking with that same easy, forward posture. However, they always show dislike by lounging back: they sit at attention for nobody, of either sex. Perhaps it's not that they never feel threatened, but that they never really learn the signals for negotiating status that men use. The experiment that produced these findings is criticized by the kinesicists because it's so far from natural observation: subjects were asked to sit down and *imagine* that they were with someone they liked or disliked. However, other research lends support, and there is logic to the results.

There is a kind of folklore about postures and how some of them can be interpreted. A woman who folds her arms across her chest, for example, comes across to many people as shy, cold, or simply passive. If her arms are down at her sides, she seems more open and accessible. Actors use such postures quite consciously. In a television show, when a suspect pleads with a detective, if the script calls for an unsympathetic response the detective is almost certain to stand with arms folded. If he doesn't, the nuances of the performance may be subtly different. In encounter groups, when in the early stages participants seem very defensive and unwilling to say what they think, they are sometimes asked to sit with arms and legs open, on the theory that this will make them *feel* more open and so behave more openly with one another. However, as always, the limbs aren't the whole message. A tilt of the head, a seductive smile, an easy slant to the shoulders—in fact, minimal body tension— and the effect of folded arms, for instance, would be rather different.

One psychiatrist, who recorded over a period of years the postures and postural shifts of patients he was treating, found that certain postures were almost predictable at particular junctures. Each patient had a basic couch position and varied it with arm and leg movements and whole-body shifts that regularly coincided with certain verbal statements. For example, a patient might have a way of holding his body when reminiscing about his mother that was quite different from his posture when talking about his father. He might hold his arms so that they shielded his chest or abdomen whenever he was feeling defensive, or thrust his hand into his pocket when feeling aggressive and masculine.

Kinesicists have begun to examine posture in a broad new context, working with films made in public places: the streets of a small town where people were gathering for a parade, a picnic ground, and a university campus. Their findings so far suggest that those who are outside the action, standing on the periphery of a group or scanning from the sidelines, in small ways hold their bodies rather differently than insiders do. Typically, they stand with weight on just one foot rather than on both, perhaps with hands propped on hips and head up or even tilted slightly back. A college freshman at a mixer, wanting to appear blasé, may strike just such a pose. Someone who's really involved in the gathering, on the other hand, will lean forward a little and tip his head forward.

Social scientists have also investigated orientation, or the extent to which two people face each other. Among the nonhuman primates, who of course have no language, this is a vitally important clue to an animal's intentions. A chimp specifies which other animals he's paying attention to by where he points his body and where he directs his gaze.

Men do the same thing, though probably in subtler ways. One individual can face another solidly with his whole body, or with just his head, or just his upper body or legs. Orientation is difficult to study, and results have been rather ambiguous, but it's likely that how solidly he faces another indicates the degree to which he is paying attention. The emotional impact is entirely different if he squares off than if he stands with his body turned out of the conversation and connects only occasionally by turning his head. In fact, you can stop a conversation cold by turning your back on it, while facing another person and turning just your head away has the same effect but takes longer.

Often, in a group of three or more, people will divide their body orientation. You will frequently see that each person has pointed the upper part of his body at one of his companions and the lower half at the other. If that didn't happen, if instead two people oriented entirely to each other, the third would feel inexplicably left out, no matter how carefully he was included in the conversation at the verbal level.

Experiments on orientation suggest that both men and women face disliked high-status men most directly, and low status women least directly. Again, threat potential seems to be important—the boss versus the cleaning woman.

Roughly one thousand static postures are both anatomically possible and relatively comfortable, and from these each culture selects its own quite limited repertoire—so reports Gordon Hewes, who has surveyed posture on a global scale. We in the West tend to forget that there are other ways to sit and stand than the ones we're accustomed to. It's a surprise to learn that "at least a quarter of mankind habitually crouches in a deep squat for rest or work." Most young children squat easily and comfortably for long periods of time, but in societies such as ours, where the deep squat is considered awkward, uncomfortable, and impolite, adults have lost the ability to do it. A culture's postural repertoire shapes its furniture and the furniture in turn requires certain postures. When a life-style is in flux, posture-to-furniture mismatches sometimes occur. In Japan, where people are used to sitting on the floor at home, one sometimes sees them squatting on their heels on top of a seat in a theater or on the train.

If squatting looks uncomfortable to Westerners, the graceful, storklike Nilotic stance assumed by men in some parts of Africa looks impossible. The men stand for long periods on one leg with the other bent at the knee, the foot of the free leg braced casually against the other leg's shin.

Hewes found, across all the cultures he studied, that it was rare for women to stand or sit with legs held apart, a posture that was common for men. And every culture had postures it considered proper and others held to be improper, though what was polite in one society could be just short of scandalous in the next.

Of all nonverbal behavior posture is, as I've said, the easiest element for the layman to observe and interpret. In a way, it's disturbing to learn that body motions we have assumed were quite random are so circumscribed, predictable, and—sometimes—revealing, but in another way it's delightful to learn that with our whole bodies we continually respond to the unfolding of any human encounter.

As an individual becomes more posture conscious, he may suddenly realize one evening that he has been sharing postures with a friend and has just gone along companionably with a postural shift; or in another situation he may become aware that he is sitting barricaded behind his own arms and legs. This kind of heightened self-awareness can be a first, tentative step toward greater self-knowledge.

Body Rhythms | 12

Like other kinesicists, Professor William Condon has
worked with films, watching and analyzing, looking for
patterns. From this research, he has become aware of a
fascinating and surprising phenomenon: in minute ways
a man's body dances continually to the beat of his own
speech. Whenever he talks, his hand and finger movements, head nods, eye blinks—all the motions he
makes—fall in with that beat. Interestingly, this rhythm
breaks down when there is pathology or brain damage.
Schizophrenics, autistic children, people with Parkin-
son's disease, mild epilepsy, or aphasia, and people who
stutter, are out of synchrony with themselves. The left
hand may go with the rhythm of the speech, while the
right is completely out of phase. The result, in films or in
real life, is a fleeting impression of awkwardness, a
feeling that something about the way the person moves is
somehow not quite right.

"After I had spent thousands of hours looking at films," Condon recalls, "I began to catch, with peripheral vision, the lock-in—the fact that the *listener* also moves in time with the speech of the speaker. So I began to examine this systematically, and that was the beginning of the study of interactional synchrony."

Interactional synchrony is hard to believe until you've seen it in films, since in life it usually happens too quickly and is too subtle to catch. But in the over a hundred films that Condon has analyzed it has always been there, whether the films were of middle-class Americans, Eskimos, or African Bushmen. It goes on continuously whenever people are involved in conversation. Even when a listener seems to be sitting perfectly still, microanalysis reveals that his eye blinks or the rate at which he puffs on his pipe synchronize with the words he is listening to. When two people talk, then, they are linked not just by the words that pass between them but by this shared rhythm. It is as if they were carried along together by the same current. Sometimes even during silence people will move together, apparently reacting to visual cues in the absence of verbal ones. It's possible to experiment with interactional synchrony using a very simple technique: ask a friend to beat out a rhythm with his finger and then talk to him. His taps will quickly begin to coincide with the stress points or the syllable divisions of your speech. Human-speech rhythms can be as irresistible, apparently, as the rhythms of hard rock.

Interactional synchrony is a subtle thing, not an exact mirroring of gestures—though that sometimes occurs—but simply a shared beat. The speaker's head may move to the right and exactly as it does so, the listener will lift one hand. At the same instant in which the head motion reverses itself, the hand will change direction. If the head speeds up, the hand will, too, or perhaps now the foot will pick up the beat or the other hand will.

One wonders, of course, what possible purpose inter-actional synchrony could serve, since people are virtually never aware of it. Condon believes it's the bedrock on which human communication is built; that without it communication might not be possible at all. What it tells the speaker is that his listener *is* listening. In fact, if the listener's attention strays, synchrony fades or cuts out altogether. Condon has a film clip of two psychiatrists talking together and moving to the same rhythm. After a while two other people arrive on the scene and the psychiatrists break off their dialogue so that each can converse with one of the newcomers. The moment they begin to pay attention to these new conversations, the synchrony between them breaks up. A few minutes later, when the doctors resume their original conversation together, mutual rhythm revives.

Interactional synchrony varies. Sometimes it's only faintly there and sometimes it's enormously heightened. Two people may sit moving just their heads in rhythm, then they may add hands or a foot waggle until soon it seems that with their whole bodies they're dancing in time. The internal experience at that moment is a feeling of great rapport, of really getting through to the other person—though the conversation may actually be completely trivial. On a subliminal level, then, interactional synchrony expresses subtle but important variations in a relationship.

It has taken eight years of incredibly patient and painstaking research to teach Condon as much as he now knows about synchrony. Throughout this time, his lab has been at Western Psychiatric Institute and Clinic in Pittsburgh, where he is an Associate Research Professor of Human Communication.

He cautioned me when I interviewed him that his findings still have to be described as "tentative." They have, he said, about the same validity as Konrad

.orenz's observations of animals in the wild. In over a hundred films Condon has corroborated his original finding, and others who have looked at the films have seen the synchrony, too, but the proof isn't in yet in statistical, experimental terms.

In a room the size of a large closet, Condon showed me a series of his films. The first was of a conversation between a white man and a black man, strangers to each other, brought to the WPIC lab and asked to sit down and talk to each other to provide data for a study in human communication. The two men, both well dressed, sat facing one another. The black man was young, a student; the white, somewhat older. Leaning back in their chairs they argued politely the respective merits of a college education (the student was for it) versus skilled labor, which the white man defended.

Condon hand-cranked the film, going over and over it for me a few frames at a time. In slow motion, the sound was sometimes very Donald Duck, sometimes more like seals barking or a wind howling, but always the cadence was clear, even when the words weren't. Gradually, I began to see that each man, when he talked, moved to his own beat; and then, suddenly, out of the corner of my eye I caught the fact that they really *were* moving together. The white man was talking and though the black was sitting rather still, each time he did move his motion coincided with the vocal stress point in a phrase the other was uttering.

Condon explained that in this early part of the film the men were arguing and there wasn't much synchrony. Divorced from their words, their gestures seemed rather aggressive as they pointed, thrust, and chopped the air. Then the white said, contradicting himself, "I want—I don't want—" and I saw his head go back, teeth bared, eyebrows raised as, in an emphatic gesture almost like a slap, he hit out at the air.

Immediately, the black man straightened right up in

his chair. From then on the whole tone of the encounter was startlingly different. Where before there had been sporadic synchrony, now the men moved together at the phrase level, the word level, even the syllable level, in a tight and intricate dance. There was an elaborate interplay of hand gestures, and once, when there had been a pause in the talk, one man began to speak and the other came in with a body motion precisely on the beat. The student reached into his pocket for his pipe and the rhythm of the gesture was as definite as "da-da-da-dum"—and as clearly matched to the other's speech.

The early part of the film, according to Condon, reveals a dominance-submission fight. It's difficult to say exactly what it was that happened at the instant of the slap, but certainly something changed. Perhaps the dominance issue was settled with that single, sharp gesture.

Condon next put on another brief swatch of film, this one showing Jane Goodall, the ethologist, with a pair of wild chimps. Squatting, Goodall reaches forward to take a bunch of bananas from one of the animals. It throws back its head, teeth bared, and slaps out at her in a sequence startlingly similar to the one in the film of the two men.

Returning to that film, Condon pointed out some of the subtle, cultural differences in the way blacks and whites use their bodies. Whenever the white man moved his head and his hands at the same time, they wagged to the same beat. With the black there was sometimes syncopation, the hands moving to a faster rhythm that was, however, still related to that of the head. At one point the student actually had one hand kicking about twice as fast as the other hand was. Whites, Condon said, find this almost impossible to do even when they try. When blacks and whites are together, he suggested, they suffer minor discomforts as each tries to adjust to subtle differences in the body motion of the other.

Researchers are beginning to find that black Americans and white ones *do* move in rather different ways. Blacks in general are faster, more subtle, and more sensitive to nonverbal nuances; and it seems that they often convey quite a lot by small-scale movements—of shoulders, hands, fingers. Several investigators have suggested that there may be important differences in eye behavior, too; that in poor black families, people look directly at one another less often than people do in middle-class white families. This would account for the fact that blacks meeting whites sometimes feel stared at, while whites feel that blacks are avoiding their eyes. Body-motion differences don't, of course, *cause* prejudice; however, it's no help to interracial relationships if blacks and whites simply don't read each other well.

Paul Byers, an anthropologist at Columbia University, had earlier shown me a film made at a nursery school. During a ten-minute sequence, one little black girl tried, by actual count, thirty-five times to catch the white teacher's eye and succeeded only four times, while a white child made contact eight times out of only fourteen tries. And it wasn't a case of favoritism. Analysis showed that the white child's timing was simply better: the little black girl kept looking at the teacher even when she was engrossed in helping another child, while the white girl saved her bids for attention, for the most part, for times when the teacher was free. Again and again in this film the teacher reached out to each of two little black girls but each try at contact turned into a near miss, either because the woman herself hesitated, as if not sure her touch was welcome, or because the child, with a slight, graceful ripple of the shoulders, shrugged off her hand. Byers believes the film demonstrates, not prejudice, but problems in interpreting body motions.

The third film clip Condon showed me was an example of heightened synchrony. A man and a woman—employer and job applicant—sat facing each other in a sequence that at normal speed seemed merely to involve rather a lot of shifting around, as the man first uncrossed and then recrossed his legs and the woman stirred in her chair. But when the film was run through a few frames at a time, their synchrony became clear. In the same frame, the two began to lean toward each other. They stopped at the same split second, both raised their heads, and then they swept backwards together into their chairs, stopping in the same frame. It was very like the elaborate courtship dances of some birds, or—in Condon's favorite analogy—they were like puppets moved by the same set of strings. Condon told me that this kind of heightened synchrony happens often between male and female. During courtship, it's one of the ways in which vast statements can be made between a man and a woman without a word being said.

Men and women may have somewhat different styles of synchrony, Condon added. In the male-male encounters he has looked at so far, the bounce and the rhythm are quite different from male-female sequences. Movements in general are damped down between men, or the two may engage in an elaborate hand dance, but not so much of the body is involved and the rhythm doesn't mesh as tightly.

"It would seem that human life is deeply involved in shared rhythmic movement with its surround," Condon has written. "The baby in the womb moves with the mother's movements. After birth the shared movement and rhythm continues . . ."

Kinesic analysis has taught Condon that even very tiny babies are self-synchronous. Though their movements seem random and jerky, all parts of the body do kick to the same beat. And by three and a half months—possibly earlier—the baby moves in rhythm with his mother's speech.

"In fact, between mother and infant there is heightened synchrony," Condon said, "very sinuous, relaxed, extensive. They lock in over long periods of time with a sharing of movement. Films of a mother chimp grooming a baby chimp show the same thing."

In the next group of films Condon showed me, there were illustrations of the kind of pathology that blocks interactional synchrony. The first film was of a beautiful little girl, a three-year-old with enormous eyes and long, dark hair. She was brought to the WPIC lab because doctors suspected that she might be deaf, though hearing tests had proved inconclusive. Condon believed that, if she had normal hearing, films would show that she moved in synchrony with the speech of others. However, instead the film showed that she moved not at all with the human voice but reacted with extreme sensitivity to inanimate sounds. Her mother lowered a bead necklace onto a table so that it collapsed in sections, making a sound like a delicate drum roll; and the little girl's head and shoulders kicked gently in time with the pattering of the beads. A child-care worker tapped on the table and she moved with the taps. Normal children don't react this way to sound. Condon has even tried loud sounds on them, such as books being slammed around, and even then they don't pick up the beat.

The little girl in the film was later diagnosed as autistic.

"Poor little thing," said Condon, "it was as if her world was composed of noises and she danced in time to those the way normal people dance with human speech."

In the next film clip, a woman in a pale halter-top dress was sitting on a sofa with a man, while in the foreground a little boy was playing on the floor. The woman was complaining to her companion about the boy, who had always been, she said, a feeding problem. In the tone of her voice, which momentarily took on a sharp, squeezed quality as she spoke of her son, and in her gestures, especially one particular angry stab of the finger, she expressed her rejection of the child. But as she talked he rose, his small body unfolding in perfect time with the rhythm of his mother's speech, and disappeared from the screen, only to reappear a few seconds later carrying a small pillow, which he offered to his mother in what seemed a gesture of atonement or appeal. But the woman took it from him with a cold, angry, closed face that I was to remember for a long time afterward.

The next film showed a mother with her twin daughters, one of whom was schizophrenic. In the whole thirty-minute film the mother and the well twin moved together and shared postures ninety-five percent of the time; they even adjusted their skirts together in the same frame of the film. The sick twin rarely shared rhythm or posture with either. In fact, the few times she did adopt her mother's posture, the mother almost immediately shifted to another one, almost as if this were a way to keep the child at a distance. And again and again as the woman spoke of her schizophrenic daughter, she gestured at her with a palm-down slapping motion that clearly said: Get away. Sometimes the girl reacted by turning her head sharply aside and withdrawing more than ever from the conversation.

"These are major messages," Condon said to me soberly. "When you've seen enough films you learn to accept them as reality."

But he cautioned that there is no simple cause-and-effect relationship here. The mother's rejection didn't cause her daughter's schizophrenia. In fact, the sick twin may have been a poor communicator from the beginning. But Condon has another film of a mother and eight-year-old twins, one normal and one not, which shows the same pattern of rhythmic and postural exclusion; and he has now also collected several films of mothers with normal twins, in all of which the mother shares pretty evenly with both children. It seems, then, that interactional synchrony can be not only a way of expressing rapport, but a way of excluding or including others.

In another film, of a troubled adolescent boy and his parents, mother and son show clearly by their behavior that they're allied against the father. In fact, at one point the boy begins to argue with his father and the mother reinforces this by immediately adopting her son's posture and moving into heightened sync with him. At another point the mother and father lock in together beautifully and the boy immediately says to his mother angrily, "Well, you just shut me off, you just turn me off now"—which provides, Condon said, further verification that there is locking out as well as locking in.

Condon speculates that catching another person's rhythm may have roughly the same effect as sharing his posture: it promotes a feeling of closeness, of rapport. People are enormously sensitive to the way other people move. Edward Hall has a collection of photographs taken in art galleries of people unthinkingly sharing the postures of sculptured figures.

People have this remarkable sensitivity and they don't even know it [Dr. Condon mused]. There may be, for all I know, several hundred different levels of being able to state closeness or distance in a relationship—with posture, synchrony, eye contact, and so on. Life gets so much more fascinating as you study this; it gets quite delightful. I think as people learn about it there will be nuances of pleasure, of shared relationship, that we know nothing about now, because our sensitivities will increase.

What is perhaps the most remarkable of all Condon's films was the last one he showed me. For it, he had two subjects wired up to an EEG—an electroencephalograph—so that he could record their brain waves as they talked. One camera focused on the human encounter, another on the pens of the EEG as they drew squiggly lines on the graph paper flowing under them. Two films resulted. On screen in the EEG film, one sees a line-up of twelve pens, the six on the right for the man, the six on the left for the woman. They look rather like a line of not very adept ice skaters, skating together to unheard music. They don't all swing left or right at the same instant, but most swing one way or the other in synchrony, and they speed up or slow down in synchrony. In an eerie way, it's almost as if the pens themselves are talking to each other.

I was reminded of a remark Paul Byers had made to me, half-jokingly: that interactional synchrony, or rhythmic relationships, may eventually provide an explanation for ESP or even for man-to-plant communication, that weird phenomenon whereby certain people, just by concentrating on a plant—perhaps by loving it a little—can make it grow considerably better than a control plant that is otherwise treated in precisely the same way, watered as often, given as much sunlight, and so on. Byers said: "What are we, after all—our actions, our perceptions—but nerves firing: rhythms?" And he suggested that when the young talk about "good vibes" and "bad vibes" they're unconsciously recognizing precisely that.

Condon himself is cautious about the EEG film. All you can say, he warned, is that it's very suggestive and a phenomenon worth exploring. But there are problems in working with EEGs. No one can say precisely what they measure except that they reflect the electrical activity of the brain, complicated by the muscle kick from eye blinks. One scientist has said that trying to explore the brain with an EEG is like trying to figure out how a car engine works by holding a stethoscope against the hood. However, Condon's EEG record appears to show complex configurations of change that relate to the speech stream and he intends to do further studies to try to "tease out" what these relationships are.

Condon is convinced that the bioelectric—the body's nervous system which works by the electrical firing of nerves—picks up interactional synchrony and is deeply involved in it. He believes that the nervous system vibrates rhythmically in response to speech, and compared the whole mechanism to two electric motors, wired up in synchrony so that if there is any change in the oscillation of one motor, the other goes right along with it. Just as the motors are connected by wires, so human beings are connected by sound.

"Humans are incredibly attuned to language and heard sound," Condon explained. "That's the highest evolved process. I believe that anything going on below that level locks in with it automatically, so that the total organism is interlocked and there's no real separation between the linguistic and the kinesic."

People apparently synchronize with others not by anticipating the pattern of their speech but by a flash reaction, rather like a reflex. In films shot at twenty-four or forty-eight frames per second the synchronization seems to be instantaneous. Matching movements start in the same frame of the film. But when a high-speed camera is used and there are ninety-six little pictures per second, a lag begins to show up between speech and gesture. It's as if the sound reaches the listener and is processed in an instant at some lower neurological level, where it makes its impact on his rhythm. Perhaps this explains why rhythm sharing almost never reaches conscious awareness.

When two people who don't speak the same language interact, there is synchronization, but of a halting, damped-down kind. Not only is the speech pattern of each unfamiliar to the other, but it's possible that on a more basic, biological level their rhythms are somewhat askew. Since speech, body motion, and EEG all seem to connect so beautifully, other physiological rhythms, such as the heart rate, may be affected, too. There's a certain amount of evidence that lends support to this theory. Various physiological rhythms, in man and animals, can be brought into phase with a metronome. And studies of humans listening to lullabies—whether German, Chinese, English, or whatever (apparently a lullabye is a lullabye in any language)—indicate that, as people listen, their breathing gradually becomes shallow and regular as in sleep, and timed to the phrase-structure of the song, while the heart rate slows and the GSR holds steady. When subjects listened to jazz under identical conditions, their breathing and GSR became irregular. Perhaps a man's basic physiological rhythms follow the rhythm of his language, so that his cadence is French or American, not just in his speech but for his whole system.

Condon, whose work has been, as he puts it, "very micro" for years, is turning to more "macro" things now. As he works with greater spans of time, he has found that certain rhythmic intervals occur so frequently that one is tempted to think them built into the organism. Very often there is a good strong beat about once a second, which approximates the human heart rate. This isn't so regular that one can write off interactional sync as simply a one-per-second twitch—the rhythmic fit in body motions is much too precise for that—but the heartbeat rhythm is often there.

The explanation for this may lie in the fact that the baby in the womb lives for nine months with the steady drumming of the maternal heart, and it has been found that, after birth, newborns allowed to listen to a recording of a human heart beating cry less and gain more weight than other babies of the same age. So it wouldn't be surprising to learn that this is a very basic human rhythm.

Adam Kendon has analyzed several films for interactional synchrony and has suggested that when two people adopt a common rhythm, it's not always a sign of great rapport or a signal that each has the other's full attention. Sometimes, it may communicate something subtler. For example, when a man begins to talk, for the first few seconds his companion may display heightened synchrony, perhaps even to the extent of exactly mirroring the speaker's gestures, indicating that he is paying close attention. Then he may settle back and sit quite still for a time, barely moving a muscle. But as soon as there are indications that his friend is winding up his statement, the listener begins to move again quite conspicuously. This time, his movements pick up the other's rhythm but don't imitate his exact gestures. Instead, almost immediately, the speaker will start to mirror the listener. By beginning to move at this juncture, the listener apparently signals that he now wants to speak. His movements may also help him to time his first word. Just as a musician will beat time with his foot while waiting to come in on the beat, humans may pick up another person's rhythm to be ready to speak the instant he finishes.

Kendon, Condon, and others involved in the study of interactional synchrony believe that there's still a lot to be learned about it. In his own work, Condon plans to move in two directions: toward microanalysis even more fine-grained, in his investigation of the nervous system, and toward macroanalysis of films of psychotherapy and family counseling. He has already turned up in these films visible evidence of the way one person may "identify" with another—a son with a father, for example, or a student with a teacher. The adolescent boy in the film mentioned earlier had acquired some of his mother's gestures, in particular a right-hand/left-hand juggling that she used when she was feeling indecisive, and the son juggled even when his mother was nowhere around. Such unconscious mimicry is very common, and one individual will often pick up a gesture, a laugh, a trick of intonation from another he admires.

"So we can begin to demonstrate identification in behavioral terms—we can find it in intonation and other vocal qualities and in body motion as well. Why, every day I pick up such identifications in the younger staff members here," Condon said, referring to bits of behavior adopted from the senior staff. "I have observed a particular gestural configuration and laugh I myself have picked up this way. Occasionally, I hear myself do it and think: Oh, damn!"

Condon's findings are used now to train psychotherapists. The young therapists watch in films, for example, the way an experienced psychiatrist reinforces a theme: the patient hits a topic that's important and the therapist leans forward and moves into heightened synchrony. Good therapists use their bodies this way instinctively and so in kinesics lessons the emphasis is on training the fledgling analysts to interpret the patient's body behavior, rather than on teaching them to manipulate their own.

At the airport on my way home from Pittsburgh, after hours of watching interactional synchrony on film, I actually caught the real thing happening in a curbside tableau. Two elderly skycaps and a vivacious blond stewardess, evidently old friends, standing close and occasionally touching, were locked in animated conversation, with heads and hands dancing beautifully together in heightened synchrony.

13 | The Rhythms of the Human Encounter

Imagine that you're being interviewed—for a job, a promotion, whatever. You've arrived, slightly on edge, but, wonder of wonders, the interviewer has turned out to be the perfect listener. He sits there, alert, courteous, giving you his undivided attention, and lets you do the talking. Every time you pause to get his reaction he's right in there with a question that tells you he very much wants to hear more. It's a good feeling.

But then suddenly everything changes. You pause and wait expectantly for the man to say something and he sits there, blank faced. The silence stretches on and on until it becomes uncomfortable. Thinking that perhaps he didn't understand, you rephrase your last remark. Still, he sits there silently. So you try another topic of conversation. You ramble on for a minute and then stop. Again: silence. Afraid to ask what's wrong, you nervously stumble into speech again. The moments drag by as you flounder, searching for something to say that will rekindle the man's interest, will earn a reply. At last, you appear to have hit on the right subject, for when you pause this time, the interviewer finally opens his mouth to ask an interested, encouraging question. But by now you're feeling hot, flushed, and unhappy and before you know it you're well launched into an angry tirade about how your last employer treated you—and about employers in general. But each time you pause now, the man comes in with a question, an expression of interest, and gradually you begin to feel calmer and to forget your earlier discomfort.

The type of interview I've just described is not in any sense an ordinary one. It is called the Programmed Interaction Interview, a complex and highly accurate diagnostic tool. Any information the subject—in this case, the imaginary "you"—supplies is totally irrelevant. Even the apparently attentive interviewer will probably remember very little of it. What matters isn't what is said but the whens and how-longs of the way it's said. Whenever the subject speaks, an observer (or the interviewer himself) records how long his remark lasts; each time he's fed a question, the observer notes how long he takes to respond.

The recording technique itself is beautifully simple. It's all done with a little black box the size of a container of kitchen matches. Though the box looks innocuous enough, it's connected to an event recorder and a computer nearby. Every time the subject speaks, the observer depresses a button on the box marked "A." Every time the interviewer speaks, he pushes the "B" button instead. The buttons also go down for head nods, smiles, and other nonverbal behavior if it seems clearly a conversational response. The end result is an exact chronological record, a kind of time chart, that shows how long and how often each person responded (or "acted," in scientific terms) and that also charts silences, interruptions, and so on. And in this record, the interviewer's behavior can be taken as a constant because he has been trained so that he knows how soon to answer, exactly how long to talk, and when and how long to remain silent.

Human beings are enormously regular in their patterns of listening and speaking. If a man who goes through this diagnostic interview is reinterviewed weeks, months, or even a year later, he will behave very similarly on the second occasion. He will speak as often, and each time he speaks he will hold the floor for approximately as long, and he will react the same way to stress. Apparently, a man's conversational rhythm is one of his more stable and predictable characteristics, and, as measured in the Programmed Diagnostic Interview, it reveals quite a lot about how he relates to other people.

Everyone uses conversational rhythms to interpret relationships. If you stop to think about it, you can characterize almost anybody you know by describing his speech pattern. One man responds only after a thoughtful pause and speaks slowly in lengthy passages as if deliberately taking time to think things out as he goes along; another leaps in to finish your thought for you, takes off on a tangent of his own, and then ends his remarks as abruptly as he began them. If you imagine the two trying to talk to one another, you can get a feeling for the way the interplay of different interaction rhythms can affect a relationship. The effects of this interplay are often far subtler than one would expect and much more predictable and, of course, they exert their influence usually at a subconscious level. Words are too much of a distraction for most of us. We're too preoccupied with what the other person says to take notice of how he went about saying it. Yet if it were possible to negate words—

to substitute nonsense syllables, for example—the meaning of the whens and how-longs would become clear.

And this, in effect, was what was done, and done very cleverly, in an experiment at Cornell University. Psychologists recruited three graduate students, gave them a topic to discuss, and then video-taped them as they sat talking. Afterwards, over a hundred "judges" were brought in. Half of them were shown the video tape, the other half saw a light show, a panel of three flashing lights with no sound. Each light represented one of the students and the three together exactly reproduced their encounter. When the first light came on, it meant that that student was speaking. If, a few seconds later, a second light flashed, he was being interrupted. Whenever no lights were on, that was silence. All the judges, once they'd seen the light show or video tape, were asked to fill in a questionnaire and one of the main questions asked was: Which student was dominant, and which, submissive? The judges who had only seen the light show had no more trouble determining that than the judges who'd seen the tape.

How much a person talks and the pattern his speech takes are important determinants of the way people react to him. Psychological studies have shown that in a group the person who does the most talking has the highest status, and is most apt to be chosen as leader. It's also true that other members of the group reserve their most ambivalent feelings for him. Someone who often interrupts is probably out to dominate; someone who leaps in eagerly when there's a break in the conversation is generally a go-getter, or in executive lingo a "self-starter." These insights are almost obvious; however, a man's interaction rhythm reveals many other, subtler characteristics as well.

The man who "discovered" interaction rhythms, and invented not only methods of measuring them but also a

computer—called an interaction chronograph—to analyze them, is an anthropologist. Dr. Eliot Chapple developed the earliest model of the chronograph in the late
nineteen thirties and used it for years to screen personnel
applicants for department stores and corporations. Since
1961 he has been director of a unit at Rockland County
Hospital that employs the chronograph to diagnose and
treat disturbed adolescents, and to evaluate adult psy-
chotics.

When I visited Rockland, a mental hospital just an
hour or so north of Manhattan, Dr. Chapple explained to
me some of the basic biology behind his work. The
human body is a vast and intricate skein of rhythms that
occur at all levels of time—from the monthly menstrual
cycle to the heart and respiratory rates, which are
measured in beats or breaths per minute, to the ten
shudders per second that constitute shivering. Most of
the body's internal systems are governed by circadian
rhythms, day-long cycles that crest once every twenty-
four hours. For each individual there is a time of day
when his body temperature is lowest, his heart rate is
slowest. Blood sugar, glandular activity, metabolism, cell
division, sensitivity to drugs, and much more, all vary
according to predictable twenty-four-hour cycles. Some
people do their best work in the morning, while others
are at their sharpest at night, because their body systems
are at peak efficiency at those times. Not surprisingly,
periods of activity and inactivity parallel other body
rhythms and also follow a day-long cycle.

Biological rhythms exist at every step of the evolutionary ladder from amoeba to man as well as in plants.
They vary from species to species, and within each
species from individual to individual, but for any given
individual they're highly regular and characteristic.
Furthermore, if a single cell is isolated from the body,
circadian rhythms can be detected in it, an indication that

the biological factors that make one person different from another begin right at the cellular level.

It's not hard to accept the fact that body temperature fluctuates according to a circadian cycle, but one finds oneself resisting the idea that interaction patterns are just as predictable. We like to think that we talk because we have something to say and stop talking when we're through saying it. Yet Chapple's years of testing literally thousands of people leave no room for doubt that the pattern is there.

It is, Chapple believes, a pattern that is partly innate. He thinks that an individual's future interaction rhythm is first manifested by how active (or inactive) that person is as a baby. However, before the rhythm becomes set at the age of three or four, experience can change it considerably. If the baby is severely stressed in his first year, there may be physiological changes within his system that will ultimately affect his interaction rhythm for the rest of his life.

Experience acts on heredity in other ways. Studies have shown that when a mother approaches a high-activity baby he relaxes, while a low-activity infant responds to his mother's approach by becoming more animated. But if the mother handles the very active baby roughly, she may overstimulate him and prevent him from relaxing, and the more placid baby will stay placid if the mother takes pains to avoid exciting him. If a mother is disappointed in her low-activity baby, or unable to cope with her high-activity infant, in each case her response is fed back into her relationship with the child, who then reacts to her reaction—and so the whole complex character-shaping process begins.

From earliest childhood an individual's basic rhythm affects his relationships with other people, so it's easy to see that throughout his life it will be important to him to find people whose interaction rhythms complement his own. Chapple says that "finding the 'perfect listener,' gaining that sense of relaxation from being able to talk or not talk when one 'wants' to, is one of the greater pleasures," but complementarity is actually rather hard to come by. Most of the people we meet operate at tempos that don't mesh with our own.

Whenever two people meet who haven't yet established a comfortable relationship, there's a period of groping for a common rhythm. At first, they may keep interrupting one another without meaning to, or one may finish a statement and catch the other unprepared, so that he lags with his response. There are nonverbal cues that signal that a person is finishing up what he has to say—tricks of eye behavior and of intonation, for example—but when a conversation runs really smoothly it's partly because the participants have arrived at a stable, mutual rhythm. This may, however, represent different things to each of them. For one it may be a natural and comfortable pattern; the other may have to strain to maintain it.

While everyone has his own particular, basic rhythm—the one that goes with the times when he's feeling particularly good or is with dear and comfortable friends—most people vary their rhythms within a certain range and in fact have a whole set of subrhythms, like harmonics in music. A man may habitually operate at one rhythm when with his wife or with old friends and at quite another when with his employer. These secondary rhythms aren't random but, surprisingly, when computer analyzed they appear to be mathematical multiples of the basic beat—a doubling or a halving, for example. Some people are very flexible and have a lot of subrhythms available. Others aren't. These are the compulsive talkers or the individuals who speak seldom and almost grudgingly.

Interaction rhythms help to explain some of the

paradoxes of human relationships—the people who appear to have everything in common who just can't seem to get along, the people who apparently have nothing in common who get along beautifully.

One of the ways husband and wife can be mismatched is in their basic interaction rhythms. This isn't always obvious during the courtship period, since at that time both are very attentive and eager to adjust. Sometimes after marriage mismatched couples seem to arrive at a stable pattern, only to have it crumble away a few years later. One couple I know had been married for two years when the wife began to complain that she could never get an answer out of her husband—he took so long to respond that she would become upset and angry as she waited. He replied that he'd never been a talkative man, and that she knew that when she married him. This was an instance in which stress was cumulative, and as it built up it caused both individuals to become more rigid and less able to adjust, until the mismatched rhythms that once hadn't mattered began to contribute heavily to their mutual discontent.

It's also true that people don't have isolated relationships with isolated others, but instead live in the midst of a whole system of relationships, so that rhythmic imbalance at one point may be compensated for by rhythmic balance at others. Thus, the man with the garrulous wife may get along all right if he's taciturn himself, or if he has enough friends who are willing to let him have his say. If he loses some of those friends, he may suddenly begin to find his marriage intolerable.

Originally, all Dr. Chapple's interaction recording was done in natural situations. He observed conversations between married couples, friends, strangers. But while it was usually possible by elaborate statistical analyses to determine any individual's basic interaction rhythm in such a situation, it was difficult to do, since each person was continually adjusting to the other. Moreover, when Chapple tried using interviewers, even skilled psychiatrists all asking the same questions, the individual was often remarkably different with each. So Chapple began to train interviewers, to program their behavior—to control for the personality factor. And he found that interviewers who were taught not only what to say but how long to take in saying it, how long to wait before responding, and how to manage their facial expressions, were able to produce accurate and consistent recordings.

And so the standardized Diagnostic Interview was developed. What it does is to record, first of all, the individual's basic beat; it then subjects him to precisely metered amounts of stress to determine his characteristic patterns of reacting. From this, it's possible to learn quite a lot about his personality and the way he relates to others.

People who go through the interview ordinarily aren't told what it's all about. The procedure is divided into five time periods and starts with fifteen minutes of complementarity—heady stuff, since Chapple's interviewers are trained to respond with perfect synchrony and flattering, single-minded interest. Then comes the period of nonresponse described at the beginning of this chapter. Each time the subject stops talking there's dead silence. For a full fifteen seconds the interviewer won't speak, unless the subject does first. This happens twelve times in all, though there is a cutoff point after fifteen minutes.

Many people equate nonresponse with withdrawal and rejection and become very shaken up when it happens repeatedly. And every individual has a characteristic way of reacting to it. Some people break the silence earlier each time it occurs with remarks that get progressively briefer. It's as if the stress speeds up their tempo, or as if they must keep prodding the other person to reply. That was the reaction of the subject (the "you") in the interview I've described. The kind of person who reacts to nonresponse by speeding up is also the kind of person who has great difficulty in delegating responsibility. Finding others too often unresponsive, he prefers to do the work himself. Other people, given the nonresponse treatment, develop a compulsion to talk. Each time the interviewer fails to speak in his turn, they rush in with remarks of their own that last longer and longer. Anger seems to be the factor that sets this off. Another common reaction is to meet nonresponse with nonresponse: to wait out the other, going into sullen, suspicious withdrawal. These reactions represent extremes. Most people have a mixed response, now speeding up the tempo, now slowing down, trying both silence and speech in an attempt to get the normal give and take of conversation established again. And then there are those fortunate individuals who are quite unaware that anything is happening.

When the period of nonresponse is over, the interviewer goes back to complementarity, to the easy, beautifully synchronized pattern of the first period. The purpose is not so much to give the subject a breather as to provide an index to just how stressed he was, since stress will show up when the rhythm of this period is compared to the rhythm of period one. Some people bounce back almost immediately, apparently little bothered by the stress, but those who show signs of it are far more common.

Once the five-minute complementarity break is over, the interviewer introduces a new pattern. The subject starts to speak and precisely three seconds later is interrupted. If he ignores this and keeps right on talking, the interviewer speaks for five seconds and subsides. Then, when the subject finishes what he was saying, he feeds him another polite question, waits three seconds and interrupts again. On the other hand, if the subject stops when interrupted the first time, the interviewer speaks for five seconds, gives the other a chance to resume what he was saying, and then interrupts again. The period ends after twelve interruptions or is discontinued after fifteen minutes.

Interrupting is, of course, an attempt to dominate; it's solid evidence of aggressiveness. People have characteristic reactions to being dominated. A few are very persistent and will talk longer and louder each time they're interrupted. What's more usual is a stepped-up tempo. The subject, broken in on, hesitates and then cuts back in himself. Each time he cuts in a little sooner, so that the tempo gets faster and faster. This kind of competition, with each person interrupting the other before he can finish what he had to say, is typical of quarreling. Another common reaction is submissiveness. If he can, the individual simply cuts and runs. If he can't, he becomes very hesitant and goes in for long pauses while summoning up something to say.

Dr. Chapple has found that the timing of an interruption is particularly important. It's more unsettling to a person to be interrupted just after he has begun to talk. Once he's well under way, he can more easily override the interrupter. However, one can chop him down, make him talk for shorter and shorter spans of time, by breaking in on him repeatedly just as he's concluding his speech. Presumably, he takes such interruptions as an expression of impatience and becomes less and less sure of himself.

The dominance or interruption period is followed by another period of complementarity, to measure once again just how far from his normal rate the subject's interaction rhythm has been pushed. Some people actually underreact. They may seem nearly normal but their pace will be a little too fast, their actions a little too short,

The Rhythms of the Human Encounter 139

and they're hard to synchronize with. We all know people like this who, in the aftermath of a fight, signal in just this way that for them the conflict isn't really over. Another common reaction is petulance: the person becomes very terse or unwilling to talk at all, and he may do this even if he has beaten back all interruptions. Others —and they're generally grudge carriers—let long intervals of silence elapse before they will answer a question. In contrast, still others talk compulsively, or become very impulsive or excited. Transient reactions to being dominated can be important. If a man has a fight with his wife and immediately afterward encounters a friend, his behavior may be so out of character that his friend in turn becomes disturbed and angry.

Chapple's interviewers and observers are carefully trained. The interviewers practice getting the durations of their actions exactly right, and they're helped out by a screen high on a wall out of sight behind the subject's head. Run by a "logic box" in the next room—a small preprogrammed computer—the screen lights up with cryptic columns of numbers that tell the interviewer exactly what stage he's at: how many interruptions he has made, how much time has passed, and so on. The final results of the Diagnostic Interview are run through a computer and expressed in nice, solid, mathematical terms.

That Chapple's chronograph *can* predict patterns of interaction has been proved, not only in his own work but in studies done by British researchers and by Joseph Matarrazzo of the University of Oregon. The conclusions about personality that he draws from these patterns are constantly being tested. In addition, Chapple's years as a business consultant provide a kind of practical proof. His work with department-store sales people is particularly to the point, since sales ability proves out in a dollars-and-cents record. Time and again in "blindfold" tests, job applicants were interviewed and predictions made about their sales potential, and then the store went ahead and hired them without knowing what had been predicted. In one store, in 115 cases, the Chapple technique was right 96.8 percent of the time when it predicted "good" sales ability; 84.5 percent of the time when it predicted "above average" sales; and in predicting failure, the technique was accurate 97.7 percent of the time. As one would expect, for borderline cases, those in the "average" class, predictions were only 61.5 percent accurate.

What Chapple found in working with department stores was that different kinds of selling require quite different personalities. The girl who stands behind a counter on the main floor sometimes needs to handle a number of customers simultaneously, so it's important for her to be able to maintain a flexible and fast interaction tempo. On the other hand, a woman who sells high fashion must wait around, making small talk, while the customer tries on clothes, and must be able to sense it when the woman responds to a particular dress, so that she can really settle down to *sell* that dress. Consequently, in high fashion a certain amount of dominance is necessary.

Chapple dealt with executive jobs in the same way, by looking at what the job holder actually needed to do in very basic interaction terms, rather than at what business lore said he needed to be like. In one case business school experts had advised that a personnel director be retrained because he didn't fit the usual criteria for what a personnel man should be: he wasn't an understanding person, able to communicate easily and so on. The firm consulted Chapple, who had the man interviewed and found that he was quite rigid and rather taciturn but that he had an incredible capacity for listening. When Chapple examined the man's job, he found that he spent eighty percent of his time dealing with union representatives, who were all quite garrulous, particularly when it came to airing grievances. As it turned out, then, the personnel director was the perfect man for his particular job because he could listen all day if he needed to and then not give an inch.

These days Chapple is using the interaction chronograph procedure to do therapy. At Rockland he and his staff work with adolescent boys who have gotten into trouble because of violent, antisocial behavior. First of all Chapple uses an interview to diagnose the problem of each patient. He may find that a particular boy simply can't take being dominated and that he reacts violently to it in the period immediately following the interruptions. So computers are used to set up a program in which carefully graded amounts of dominance are applied in individual interviews and in group sessions, until the boy learns to recognize the stress and his own reaction to it and to control that reaction. In general, Chapple has found that most boys are able to manage such stress after about twelve interviews and, most important, that the learning does carry over to nontraining situations. This highly pragmatic therapy, aimed at changing behavior rather than at supplying insight, is embedded in a whole program of school lessons and sheltered workshops, where the boys earn money for piecework, and halfway houses to try to ensure that once they're back in the community they won't be overwhelmed by the same problems that sent them to Rockland in the first place.

And such approaches are also carried out in the community itself—in home, school, and neighborhood. In one special project in the Bronx, Chapple interviewers equipped with a portable recorder are following adolescents around as they go about their everyday lives, sampling interactions as they happen. From diagnostic interviews, Chapple already knows what kinds of stress disturb the boys; now he wants to record that stress as it occurs, to see when and how often it happens and how it affects them, to look at all the relationships that make up their total communication networks, and then to relate these findings to the original diagnostic interviews.

It's not easy to relate Chapple's work to what's being done by other communication scientists. For one thing, his research seems to occupy a niche that's somewhere between the verbal and the nonverbal. For another, he focuses not on a code but on the individual and on the way individual differences in basic, biological rhythm are played out in face-to-face encounters. But this basic biology is one of the easiest ways of measuring, predicting, and solving some of the practical problems of human communication.

Communicating by Smell

The verbal and the visible—what a man says and how he moves his body—are only two of the more obvious forms of communication. Humans also communicate by touch, smell, and, on rare occasions, even taste, and these senses can form an important part of the total message—yet we know much less about them.

Americans sadly underestimate the importance of the nose as a message receiver—in fact, we're so reluctant to smell one another that we may actually suppress our sense of smell. Undeniably we're an overdeodorized society, and it seems that every year advertisers discover new odors that are candidates for banishment. We live in fear of bad breath, body odor, house odors, genital odors—though any self-respecting animal knows that genital odors are pleasant and an asset in sex relations. There also seems to be a determined attempt to replace the banished natural odors with manufactured ones, with perfumes, shaving lotions, and the like. One must admit that there's something more than a little bit ludicrous about a woman who painstakingly scrubs off her own biological scent, dutifully deodorizes her body's every nook and cranny, and then annoints herself with a perfume concocted largely from the musky sex scent of some other, wiser mammal.

Why are Americans so worried by human odors? Probably it's our antisensual bias: we're suspicious of the pleasures of the senses, because they are part of the pleasure of sex. Yet of all the experiences that impinge upon us, noise and smell are the two that are irresistible. An individual can close his eyes, he can refuse to touch or to eat, but he has trouble shutting out the noises of others and it's impossible to shut out their smell. Margaret Mead has suggested that the famous ethnic mix of the United States may be partly to blame for the American odor phobia. In this country, very different groups of people who eat differently, live differently, and even sleep differently, live in close proximity, often with poor ventilation. Alien smells seem to be harder to take, and Americans have long been sensitive to them. In early pioneer reports the men who moved on west often complained not only that they felt crowded by the sight of another man living on the next hill, but that the smell of his cooking offended them, carried by the wind perhaps from two or three miles away.

Not all cultures are so antiodor. The Arabs, according to Edward Hall in *The Hidden Dimension*, "apparently recognize a relationship between disposition and smell. The intermediaries who arrange an Arab marriage usually take great precautions to insure a good match. They may even on occasion ask to smell the girl and will reject her if she 'does not smell nice,' not so much on esthetic grounds but possibly because of a residual smell of anger or discontent." Furthermore, Hall continues, "To the

Arab good smells are pleasing and a way of being involved with each other. To smell one's friend is not only nice but desirable, for to deny him your breath is to act ashamed. Americans, on the other hand, trained as they are not to breathe in other people's faces, automatically communicate shame [to the Arab] in trying to be polite."

On Bali, when lovers greet one another, they breathe in deeply in a kind of friendly sniffing. And among the Kanum-irebe tribe of Southern New Guinea, when close friends part, the one who is to remain behind will sometimes reach into the armpit of the one who is leaving and take some of his friend's odor to rub on himself.

The sense of smell is enormously important to most animals. It tips them off to the presence of enemies, excites them in the presence of the opposite sex, serves as a territorial marker, enables them to follow the herd if they become separated from it, and identifies the emotional states of other creatures. The olfactory sense even works well in sea water: it's said to be what leads salmon home to spawn. But man doesn't have as acute a sense of smell as many other animals do. As a tree-climbing creature he came to rely on his eyes rather than on his nose. Hall suggests that man's lesser keenness may actually be a blessing:

It may have endowed man with greater capacity to withstand crowding. If humans had noses like rats, they would be forever tied to the full array of emotional shifts occurring in persons around them. The identity of anyone visiting a home and the emotional connotations of everything that took place in the home would be matters of public record so long as the smell persisted. Other people's anger would be something we could smell. The psychotic would begin to drive all of us mad, and the anxious would make us even more anxious. To say the least, life would be much more involved and intense. It would be less under conscious control, because the olfactory centers of the brain are older and more primitive than the visual centers.

Recently, scientists have suggested that humans may be, without knowing it, in something like the predicament Professor Hall described. Dr. Harry Wiener, a physician with the Pfizer Laboratories in New York, has set forth a fascinating and somewhat startling theory: that men perceive odors beyond those they're consciously aware of perceiving—that there is, in fact, an olfactory subconscious.

"Odors" is perhaps a misleading word. Wiener refers to them as "external chemical messengers," or ECMs, and they include amino acids and steroid hormones—not substances in which we ordinarily detect a scent, at least in the small quantities excreted by the body. Yet they *are* excreted and can be carried in the air to enter another person's body by way of his nose.

ECMs called pheromones are enormously important in animals. The word *pheromones* was first used about ten years ago to describe the odoriferous sex attractants of insects, but it's now known that most animals excrete them and that they affect the behavior of other members of the same species. They're especially important where sex is concerned, as experiments with mice have demonstrated. If thirty female mice are confined together, each one's estrous cycle, or the cycle of periods in which the mouse is "in heat," becomes chaotic. Add just one male mouse and all the estrous cycles snap back to normal—except that they now operate in synchrony. And if a pregnant female mouse is exposed for just a quarter of an hour a day to a male mouse other than the one that impregnated her, her pregnancy will terminate; that pregnancy can also be arrested by exposing her to an empty cage just vacated by a strange male—which proves that it's the scent of the male that's crucial. And there's further proof in the fact that destroying the olfactory lobe in the brain of the female makes her immune to this kind of pregnancy blocking.

It has been suggested that, at least among animals, the external secretions of one individual can act directly on the body chemistry of another, probably on the endocrine glands. This might explain why, in conditions of extreme overcrowding, animals begin to behave in bizarre ways and eventually to die off: bombardment of the endocrine glands, especially the adrenal gland, may cause extreme stress, and may actually act in the interests of the survival of the species as a population-controlling device.

It is, of course, dangerous to generalize from animals to humans, but scientists have been intrigued by a rather startling fact turned up by Dr. Martha McClintock of Harvard when she studied the menstrual cycles of women students living in a college residence. She found that the cycles of close friends were synchronized just as they are in mice. And it was not, apparently, just a matter of the power of suggestion or of similar living habits; physical propinquity seemed to be the key to it, or in other words, the same kind of chemical transmission seen in mice may have been at work.

That man emits ECMs seems clear, but we generally assume that only dogs and other sharp-nosed animals can pick them up. As most people know, dogs can detect fear, hate, or friendship in man and they can track a man, given his scent from an article he has touched— indicating that every human has a kind of olfactory signature. (Interestingly, dogs can discriminate only with difficulty between identical twins.) It also seems clear that man excretes hormones. Police dogs, given the scent of progesterone, were able to sniff out rods that had been held by pregnant women or by women in the second half of the menstrual cycle, at both of which times the progestrone level goes up. Mosquitoes, too, respond to human odors and it has been demonstrated that they *are* actually attracted to some people more than to others. And any woman is most attractive to mosquitoes from the thirteenth to the eighteenth days of her menstrual cycle, when her estrogen level is highest.

Most animals emit sex-attracting odors and it seems certain that humans do, too. However, in animals they act as "releasers," almost automatically triggering the sex drive, while in humans the biological reaction can be overlaid with a learned one. To some few people, the smell of rubber is sexy—because of the association with condoms. To others, the natural, biological odors of the body may actually be off-putting, even threatening.

A consideration of man's anatomy supplies further evidence of a system for ECM emission. As Wiener summed it up, "The fact is that our skin does contain a profusion of odor glands which rivals that of other animals. . . . They cover our body from head to toe; their structure is extremely complex; and there are so many individual types that complete anatomic classification has never been achieved."

It seems unlikely that all those human scent glands have survived thousands of years of evolution for the benefit of dogs and mosquitoes.

Though ECMs are probably excreted in urine, stools, saliva, tears, and on the breath, Wiener believes that the bulk of them are carried by sweat, which is notoriously responsive to emotional tension and so would make an excellent signaling device.

Wiener makes a strong case for the hypothesis that humans emit ECMs; that we also *receive* them is harder to demonstrate. He cites experiments in which individuals were exposed to certain chemicals. Though the subject didn't perceive an odor, his galvanic skin response dropped within seconds and there were lesser changes in blood pressure, breathing, and heart rate.

People don't talk much about what they smell—in our culture such discussions are felt to be somehow unsavory—so no one knows how many individuals of real olfactory talent may live quietly among us, their ability unrecognized. I happened to mention once to an old and close friend that I was doing research on the sense of smell and she then admitted to me, cautiously, that she herself seems to have a much sharper nose than most people do. Her sheets, she said, have to be washed in a particular detergent or the smell annoys her. She distinguishes quite clearly between the odor men give off and the one women do, and in college used to feel terribly sorry for her roommate because "poor Betsy smelled like a man." She treasures—and never wears—an ancient cardigan because it still smells faintly of her grandmother and the scent is the biological scent of the old woman herself, not, as in romantic novels, a whiff of lavender or lilacs or some other perfume that she wore. My friend almost never admits to what she regards as her idiosyncrasy, because if she talks about it people think she's peculiar.

The sense of smell varies not only between individuals but also between the sexes. There are certain musklike scents that women can smell, though men and preadolescent girls miss them completely. A woman's sense of smell varies with her menstrual cycle and is at its height in mid-month, when her estrogen level is highest—at the time of ovulation. In fact, scientists studying olfaction have suggested that, as a simple birth-control measure, it might be possible to use the female olfactory cycle as a tip-off to ovulation.

It's very possible that some, perhaps all, children in

our culture start life with a very sharp sense of smell and then learn to suppress it. I've come across one piece of anecdotal evidence: A young father who complained that he was unable to bottle-feed his tiny son as long as his wife remained in the same room—apparently because the baby smelled his mother's milk and preferred it. Observers have also noted that during the oedipal phase, when father and son are in competition, little boys show a marked interest in the sexual odors of adults, and a distaste for odor of Dad.

We have so far been talking mostly about olfactory abilities that are within the normal range. However, there have also been reports for centuries of people with extraordinary ability—the true prodigies—men and women who could distinguish one person from another just by sniffing, who could detect emotions by their scent, who could tell where a friend had been or who he'd been with by the odors he carried away with him on his clothes and skin. Wiener suggests that these people were only remarkable because they were able to do consciously what most of us may often do subconsciously.

The ECM theory could explain why emotions are sometimes so contagious in crowds. It also suggests an explanation for the fact that women have a sharper sense of smell at the time of ovulation: With this extra acuteness, they're better able to pick up the sex-attractant ECMs of men. And Wiener believes that ECMs may explain some types of schizophrenia. Very little is known about the causes of schizophrenia, but some of the experts have emphasized the fact that it often involves perceptual disorders—weird visual experiences and sometimes a heightened sense of smell. And it has long been known that schizophrenics, unless they're completely out of contact with reality, have a way of perceiving with startling accuracy the secret emotions of those around them. It has also been widely reported that they have a particular smell about them—rats can differentiate between the odor of a schizophrenic and that of a nonschizophrenic and so can some humans—and a St. Louis research team has isolated the chemical, trans-3-methyl-2-hexenoic acid, that causes this smell.

Wiener's schizophrenia theory is too complex to explain in detail here, but one of his main suggestions is that some (but not all) schizophrenic patients not only emit abnormal ECMs but consciously perceive the ECMs of other people. Wiener believes that, if there *is* chemical communication between humans, then the schizophrenic may be aware of its effects. If at the same time he can't identify its nature, then he will have to conclude that it's some outside force acting upon him. He *knows* sometimes what people are feeling but he doesn't know how he knows it and they will often deny it. He is, in Wiener's analogy, like the hero of H. G. Wells' story "The Country of the Blind"—able to perceive something that people around him can't even imagine, and consequently thought to be mad or dangerous. His problems may be complicated by the fact that his own abnormal ECMs are perceived subconsciously by those around him, who find them disturbing or even frightening.

G. Groddeck, an early associate of Freud's, once wrote that: "I know, in spite of all learned teaching to the contrary, that man is primarily a 'nose-animal,' and that he only represses his acute sense of smell during childhood because life would otherwise be unbearable." And for the schizophrenic, it seems, life is. Groddeck's contention that man is a "nose-animal" is, of course, an extreme position.

Wiener notes that ECMs are just one channel of communication and ordinarily a minor channel compared to sight and sound. And his theory is, as he says, just a theory so far; however, the New York State Journal of Medicine took it seriously enough to run his three long articles describing it, several other scientific and lay journals have reported it favorably, and now other scientists are beginning to concern themselves with some of the same phenomena.

Though the evidence for an olfactory subconscious is so far pretty inconclusive, it's a fascinating possibility. There can be no doubt that most of us *do* underestimate the significance of the sense of smell, perhaps because it's in some way threatening. Odors have an almost legendary ability to trigger strong memories. And, of course, willy-nilly, sex and smell seem to go together: one could ask for no better proof of this than the energy our still in some ways puritanical society puts into its vain attempt to annihilate the natural odors of the human body.

Communicating by Touch | 15

Not only are Americans reluctant to smell one another, they are also not much given to touching. Yet touch has a special kind of immediacy, for when one person touches another the experience is completely and inevitably mutual. Skin contacts skin, directly or through layers of clothing, and there's instant awareness on both sides. That awareness is actually heightened when such contact is rare.

Touch hasn't been studied as extensively as other channels of communication have, but cross-cultural comparisons have been made, a few psychological experiments have been done, and quite a bit of information has been turned up by researchers interested primarily in other matters. What is known about touch has been beautifully pulled together twice: once fifteen years ago in a monograph by Lawrence K. Frank, and once very recently in a fascinating book by Ashley Montagu.[1]

What a man experiences through his skin is more important than most of us realize. As proof, there's the surprising size of the tactile areas of the brain, both the sensory and motor regions. The lips, the index finger, and the thumb, especially, take up a disproportionate amount of cerebral space. One might, of course, expect that the skin, as the largest organ in the body, would have considerable representation in the brain. However, the general rule in neurology is that it's not the size of the organ itself that counts, but the number of functions that the corresponding region of the brain must perform. Tactile experience, then, can be assumed to be both complex and highly significant.

Skin, as Frank pointed out, is "the envelope which contains the human organism." As such, it's sensitive to heat, cold, pressure, and pain, though just *how* sensitive it is can vary with the emotional state of the individual and with the area of the body concerned. Any human body has erogenous zones, ticklish zones, and calloused places that are virtually insensitive.

Every human being is in constant contact with the outside world through his skin. Though he isn't usually aware of it unless he stops to think about it, there is always, at the very least, the pressure of pavement against the soles of his feet, or if he's sitting, the pressure of chair seat against buttocks. In fact, the whole of the environment impinges on him through his skin; he feels air pressure, wind, sunlight, fog, sound waves—and, sometimes, other humans.

Touch is probably the most primitive of the senses: far down on the evolutionary scale, small, blind creatures

[1]Lawrence K. Frank: "Tactile Communication" in *Genetic Psychology Monographs*; and *Touching, The Human Significance of Skin*, by Ashley Montagu.

feel their way through life. And the earliest, the most elemental, and perhaps the predominating experience of the unborn human is apparently the tactile one. When an embryo is less than eight weeks old, before it has eyes or ears and while it still measures less than an inch from the top of its head to its miniscule buttocks, it responds to stroking. Tickle it lightly on the upper lip or about the nose and it will bend neck and trunk as if to get away from the tickling.

Curled securely within the uterus, the fetus feels against the whole surface of its body the warm, even pressure of the amniotic fluid and, magnified by the fluid, the steady, rhythmic thrust of the mother's heartbeat. At birth the baby is squeezed slowly and inexorably from this warm and pulsating place, subjected for a time to great pressure, and then forced out into the outside world to feel on its skin for the first time the pull of gravity, the pressure of the atmosphere, and a temperature that is not body temperature. "Skin shock," as Margaret Mead has called it, is one of the major shocks of birth. She suggests that, because the skin of the human female seems generally to be more sensitive than that of the male, men and women may begin to experience the world somewhat differently with that first moment of birth.

The baby explores by touch. That's how he discovers where his own body ends and the outside world begins. When he starts to move around, his tactile sense is his earliest guide. He comes up against surfaces that resist him and surfaces that give way, against warmth and cold, roughness and smoothness. Soon he can connect visual to tactile experience: when he sees a wall, he knows it's hard. Eventually, he will take his education one step further by learning the symbol, the word *hard*. If a baby is deprived of that first experience of learning through touching, he may not grasp the end product, the symbol, as clearly—which may help to explain why institutionalized babies sometimes have problems with abstract thought. Emotional learning begins with touching, too. The mother's voice comes to substitute for her touch and her facial expressions and gestures to communicate to the baby the same things she once communicated by the way she held him.

As the baby grows older, he learns that there are objects, and parts of himself and of other people, that are touchable, and others that aren't. Throughout the childhood years, masculine and feminine roles are learned in part as rules about what areas of the skin can be exposed, what parts of the body can be touched, and in what circumstances, and by whom.

At the age of about five or six in our society, children begin to touch and be touched less often, but at puberty they seem to become avid once again for skin contact, turning first to contact with friends of the same sex—and for boys that often seems possible only in the context of body-contact sports—and then to the opposite sex.

When the individual discovers sex relations, he is actually rediscovering tactile communication—in fact, part of the intense emotion of the sex experience may be due to this harking back to a more primitive and powerful means of expression. Between mother and child there can be almost a language of touch and the same is true in lovemaking. Furthermore, in sex relations not only is there the contact itself but the very texture of the skin is part of the experience. The anthropologist Edward Hall once wrote, "The hardened, armorlike resistance to the unwanted touch, or the exciting, ever-changing textures of the skin during love-making and the velvet quality of satisfaction afterward are messages of one body to another that have universal meanings."

This sensitivity to touch continues into adulthood, despite what has been written about the tactile poverty of the American culture. Although it's often said that we don't touch one another enough, Erving Goffman objects: "The theory that American middle class people don't touch each other when they talk is nonsense. People are handling each other all the time, but we read it out. You've got to keep your eyes open to see it."

What helps us to read it out is the fact that people generally touch at the particular place in the flow of events where the gesture can have one, and only one, meaning. For example, if a man meets a family—man, woman, and child—on a narrow sidewalk, it's perfectly all right for him to take the woman's arm in squeezing by her. She has ample protection and it's obvious that all he wants is to get by with the least amount of body contact. They are, in short, simply units in a street-traffic system and not potential social acquaintances. Or if a conversation is interrupted, the person who turns aside to deal with the interruption may casually put his hand on his companion's arm, since the gesture occurs when it can be read as a "hold" and it's clearly just part of the machinery for managing conversation.

"In a public place," Professor Goffman suggests, "you could set up circumstances so that any stranger could with impunity touch anyone you designate simply by slotting in his behavior correctly."

In any attempt to interpret touch, the slot—the context—is obviously all-important. To be taken by the hand in a reception line, for example, means nothing, though not to be taken by the hand in the same situation might be a shattering experience. The part of the body touched is also significant: a hand that rests lightly on the forearm has a rather different impact than one that rests lightly on the knee.

Touch is involved with status, too. Anyone can touch a child, and a doctor may lay hands casually on a nurse or the nurse on a patient, but let the patient—or the nurse—reach for the doctor and it's a different matter. Between people who know each other, whether an individual is in the habit of touching or not will affect the message he sends. And then there's the quality of the touch: the skin may be warm or cold, damp or dry, the contact rough and insistent, gentle and lingering, or openly sensual. In fact, the nature of the contact and the quality of the skin itself actually interact: to be stroked, however lovingly, with a damp, ice-cold hand would hardly be pleasant.

Touching—at least of an impersonal sort—goes on all around us whether we see it or not, but the very fact that we read it out in so many situations indicates something about our attitude toward it. We connect physical contact with sex, except when it's perfectly clear that there is no connection, and so we use it sparingly to express warmth and affection. On American streets, one doesn't see men walking arm in arm with men, or women with women. This is a common enough custom in South America, but to Americans it smacks of homosexuality. Even parents and their grown children often have only the most perfunctory contact.

A few years ago, Sidney Jourard, a Florida psychology professor, became interested in the question of who touched whom and where. He presented several hundred college students with charts of the human body on which twenty-two numbered zones had been mapped, and asked each student to indicate which zones on his (or her) own body had been touched for any reason by his mother, his father, his closest friend of the same sex, and closest friend of the opposite sex. Jourard also asked the students to indicate which body zones they themselves touched on the same people. He found that both male and female students touched and were touched by parents and same-sex friends only on a very few parts of the body—mostly hands, arms, and shoulders. But with the opposite-sex friend he reported, "It was almost as if the flood-gates were opened. There was a virtual deluge of physical contact, all over the body. But there was much variability in these findings. Not all the students enjoyed a steady relationship with someone of the opposite sex, and these poor devils reported that they were virtually untouched, and out of touch."

It appears that the young American, unless he is involved in regular lovemaking, is unlikely to experience his own body as it feels when someone else is touching, hugging, poking, or massaging it. Even barbers these days tend to use an electric vibrator to depersonalize the contact of hand on scalp. Jourard believes that all this confirms R. D. Laing's diagnosis of modern man as "unembodied "—our bodies tend to disappear from our experience.

It seems that both encounter groups and the drug culture are partly attempts to get in touch with the body again. In encounter groups, participants are told to touch one another, are taught to become more aware of their own bodies and those of others; and the psychedelic drugs open the individual up to a whole tide of sensations and strange perceptual experiences.

Behavioral scientists sometimes speak these days of a phenomenon called skin hunger. And certainly the young in their great, ritual gatherings at places such as Woodstock seemed to need and take comfort in what one man has called "the warmth of assembled animal bodies." But Paul Byers, the anthropologist, speculates that it's actually the old who suffer most from skin hunger in our society. They're touched perhaps less than anyone—in fact, it sometimes seems as if people are afraid old age might be contagious—and this literal loss of contact must add greatly to the old person's sense of isolation.

Ours isn't the only culture in which touching is pretty much taboo. The English and English Canadians carry untouchability further than Americans do, and Germans are still more hands offish. On the other hand, the Spanish, Italians, French, Jews, Russians, French Canadians, and South Americans are all highly tactile peoples. Within the United States, it's the citizens of Anglo-Saxon origin who are truly nontactile; the second-generation Italian, for example, in general preserves the body-contact patterns of his parents and grandparents.

Touch, taste, and smell are the close-range senses. Hearing and sight, on the other hand, can offer experience from a distance. Perhaps for this reason, their pleasures are felt to be fairly cerebral and admirable, at least in comparison to the close-range senses. As Ray Birdwhistell has pointed out, Americans tend to think in dichotomies anyway (black/white; good/bad; verbal/nonverbal) and often insist on making an illogical distinction between mind and body. Inevitably, they consider the products and perceptions of the mind as good and clean and trustworthy, while those of the body are regarded with suspicion and dislike. Bad smells, bad tastes, something with a bad or slimy feel to it—all evoke the strongest disgust; but the good smells, tastes, and the good feelings are also apt to be distrusted. Mainly, what seems to be behind the taboo is the old connection between the close-range senses and sex—which is, after all, the most close-range experience of all.

The hedonists among us will undoubtedly conclude that the bodily pleasures are in for an American renaissance, thanks to the sexual revolution. However, I doubt whether revolutionizing sexual behavior will automatically revolutionize the tactile habits of the culture. In a way, touching is even more basic than lovemaking—certainly, there are more opportunities for it. And as long as American child-rearing practices involve a limited amount of mother-child body contact, adult tactile behavior seems unlikely to change significantly. Ours is, alas, a sexual but not really a sensual culture.

The Lessons of the Womb

16

Man isn't born with words in his mouth. His earliest experience of the world around him and his earliest communications with it are necessarily nonverbal. He learns by looking, by touching, by being held, the first and possibly the most important lessons of his life. And these lessons actually begin before birth, while the baby still inhabits the womb.

By the time an infant is born, it has already experienced light and darkness, since it is dim but not pitch black in the womb. It has learned to sip liquids—practicing on the amniotic fluid sometimes to the point of hiccups—and perhaps to suck its thumb. It has acquired the knack of adjusting to the mother's body movements and it may also scratch, cringe, or stretch when bumped around or prodded.

Safe in its own aquatic world, the unborn baby feels

the warmth of the amniotic fluid against its skin, and listens in on the inner workings of the mother's body. Dr. Joost Meerloo has described the womb as a "rhythmic soundworld" because from the first dawning of awareness the fetus lives with the steady drumming of the maternal heart, syncopated with the thumping of the baby's own heart, which beats about twice as fast. The unborn itself moves rhythmically within the womb: floating, rocking, sometimes almost dancing in the early months while there's still room to move freely. When in later life people react almost ecstatically to the sound of hard rock or to jazz, it may be because they've been briefly transported back to the lost paradise of the womb. William Condon's discovery that people constantly move in rhythm with one another—that, in fact, tiny infants can be seen to move in synchrony with their mothers— suggests that this first prenatal experience with human rhythms may affect us for the rest of our lives.

"The unborn baby is capable of learning at a very fast rate," the fetologist, Dr. H.M.I. Liley, has written, and she goes on to point out, that the fetus hears a very great deal:

> The womb, we have found, is an extremely noisy place. The unborn is exposed to a multiplicity of sounds that range from his mother's heartbeat and her voice to outside street noises. Especially if his mother has not gotten too plump, a great many outside noises come through to the unborn baby quite clearly: auto crashes, sonic booms, music. And the rumblings of his mother's bowel and her intestines are constantly with him. If she should drink a glass of champagne or a bottle of beer, the sounds, to her unborn baby, would be something akin to rockets being shot off all around.

Because amniotic fluid is a better sound conductor than air, the mother's conversations are quite audible to her unborn child. In fact, Dr. Henry Truby—Professor of Pediatrics, Linguistics, and Anthropology at the University of Miami—has made the fascinating suggestion that language learning may actually begin in the womb. Extensive research done in Stockholm by Dr. Truby and colleagues proved not only that the unborn can hear *in utero* throughout at least the entire last half of the fetal term, but that a fetus in the fifth month of prenatal life is able to cry if born prematurely. There has even been a report of crying before birth. An air bubble injected into the uterus of a pregnant woman became lodged over the face of her unborn child and he apparently took an untimely gulp of air, for his thin, muffled wailing was clearly heard issuing from her abdomen. Since hearing and crying are precursors of speech, Dr. Truby feels that it isn't at all farfetched to think that the fetus' linguistic environment in its last three or four months of prenatal life has an influence on its language and speech performance in childhood. Specifically, he speculates that if, just before or just after birth, the infant were transferred to a different linguistic environment—from a place where everyone spoke Chinese, for example, to one where everyone spoke American English—then when the child began to talk, even though from the moment of birth he might never again have heard a word of his "mother" tongue spoken, there would still be subtle differences in his speech performance, detectable, if not by the naked ear, by an instrument that does sound analysis. Dr. Truby has spent fourteen years in research on neonatal cry-sound analysis. Already, he can make predictions from his birth analysis about brain damage and other developmental defects, and even about personality and performance. Prior to interviews with children whom he had recorded at birth as much as ten years earlier, he has been able to predict accurately a number of things about these children even though he was about to meet them essentially for the first time. With only the birth recording to go on, he could anticipate in a general way whether a child would be energetic or lackluster. And in one case he knew in advance just from the cry sound that the child had a cleft palate and was mentally a little slow.

The possible importance of prenatal language learning is suggested by the work of a Paris clinic which for at least ten years has been treating speechless children, youngsters of three and four who have never produced intelligible speech. Each child sits with a therapist in a small, quiet room and listens to his mother's voice, as recorded earlier by a contact microphone placed against her abdomen while she talked normally and audibly. To the adult ear, this simulation of "womb-filtered" speech sounds blurry and strange, but it has had an astonishing effect on some of the children. Some have suddenly begun to talk intelligibly, or are able to draw pictures, or both—things they've never been able to do in their lives before. Severe learning disabilities have been abated. Dr. Truby, who first visited the clinic in 1962, agrees with the opinion of its director, Dr. Alfred Tomatis, that it's as if the children have been taken back to travel a route they had somehow previously by-passed. "Retraveling" exercises have also been used to treat other aspects of arrested development in children. Schizophrenic youngsters, for example, have been put back into diapers, bottle fed, held and rocked—no matter how old or how big they were. Psychoanalysis itself is a kind of retraveling.

All of this makes one wonder about the prediction—by Dr. Bentley Glass, former president of the American Association for the Advancement of Science—that by the end of the century some humans will be gestated in the laboratory rather than in the womb. Even assuming that scientists can reproduce the chemical environment of the womb exactly, one wonders whether they shouldn't pay close attention to the sensory environment as well. And if they can't, or simply don't, what sort of child might the test-tube baby become?

Being born is a shock for the young human, perhaps the greatest shock he will ever have to cope with. If he emerges into an environment similar in many ways to the womb he has just been expelled from, the shock obviously is lessened. Yet in our culture little effort is made to ease the baby's adjustment by supplying him with some of the comforts of prenatal life. In his fascinating book, *Touching*, Ashley Montagu argues that this may be a serious mistake.

In the womb, the baby is enfolded and supported—in fact pressed in on from all sides—within the warmth of his mother's body. What most closely approximates this experience in the outside world is being held in his mother's arms. However, in most American hospitals the newborn is taken from his mother right after birth and placed in a bassinet on a flat, open surface that gives him no support at all.

Whenever his mother moves around, the unborn baby is gently rocked, and the steady drumming of her heart is always with him. But at birth, he is suddenly assaulted by a flood of new sensations that are strange, overwhelming, and—perhaps most important—random. Gone are the comforting, unchanging rhythms of his prenatal existence. Sometimes, however, newborn babies have, as an experiment, been allowed to listen to tape-recorded heartbeats, and in general, they have gained more weight and cried less than infants who weren't exposed to the heartbeat sound. They also breathed more deeply and regularly and had fewer digestive and respiratory problems.

Most women seem to understand instinctively the need for rhythmic experience and will automatically rock and pat their babies. Furthermore, when a mother rocks her child, she tends to move in rhythm with her own or the baby's breathing, and when she pats him the pats often reproduce the mother's heart rate or his. The cradle, now rarely used, once provided similar rhythmic reassurance. Until the very end of the nineteenth century, it was considered almost indispensable. However, in the eighteen nineties child-care experts began to attack it as habit forming and to condemn rocking as a "vicious practice." Eventually, the comforting cradle was replaced by the flat, dull, shelterless expanse of the crib. Montagu argues passionately for the revival of the cradle.

Montagu also believes that the American infant isn't touched and held enough. For many mammals, early tactile experiences are literally life giving. The newborn animal is thoroughly licked and groomed immediately after birth and at frequent intervals thereafter, and this isn't so much a sanitary measure as a necessary tactile stimulus. The skin is massaged, and the sensory impulses feed into the central nervous system and prime the respiratory centers and other functions. Such priming *is* a necessity: the unlicked newborn is very likely to die. Montagu suggests that in humans the prolonged contractions of the uterus that constitute labor do the same job that licking after birth does in other animals: they start the internal systems functioning.

However, the need for tactile stimulation doesn't end a few days after birth. Harry Harlow's famous experiments prove that, at least for monkeys, continued skin-contact experiences are extremely important. Harlow separated infant monkeys from their mothers soon after birth and isolated each in a cage with two inanimate mother substitutes. When one of these was a wire figure that periodically supplied milk and the other was made of soft terrycloth, the baby monkeys didn't, as one might expect, become attached to the milk-giving wire "mother." Instead, they clearly preferred the terrycloth figure and went to it for comfort—much more often between meals than they went to the wire figure. Body contact, apparently, was at least as necessary to them as food.

Body contact is also important to infant humans. Tiny babies separated from their mothers shortly after birth and placed in an institution sometimes grow up suffering from a syndrome called "maternal deprivation." For these children, mental and emotional and even physical growth is stunted. The institutionalized infant is too quiet, and sleeps too much. From the time he is five to eight months old, he tends to spend a lot of time comforting himself with monotonous self-rocking, the kind of rocking normal adults do when overcome by grief. The unmothered infant even reacts differently to being held. Two scientists who did a study of such babies wrote that: "They did not adapt their bodies well to the arms of the adults, they were not cuddly, and one noted a lack of pliability. . . . They felt something like sawdust dolls; they moved, they bent easily at the proper joints, but they felt stiff and wooden." Like the infant animal, the infant human apparently needs to have his nervous system stimulated in certain ways if he's to develop normally.

Though few American children these days suffer from maternal deprivation, Montagu, for one, believes that even normal babies in our culture don't get enough tactile stimulation. Certainly, when compared to the way children are treated in other cultures, American infants are touch poor. Balinese babies, for example, spend their days tucked into a sling that's worn everywhere by the mother, father, or some other person. At night, they sleep in an adult's arms. The Netsilik Eskimo mother keeps her baby, naked except for a diaper, on her back, snuggled down inside her parka, which is belted so that it provides a kind of carrying pouch. In the United States, in contrast, the infant is pushed around in a carriage, strapped periodically into a car seat or infant chair, or left to his own devices in a mobile-bedecked crib or playpen. When he sleeps, he sleeps alone. This early physical separation of baby and mother in our culture probably contributes to a feeling of separateness in the adult, separateness felt even within the family.

Montagu hasn't much that's good to say about child-rearing practices in the Western world. In fact, he believes that the tactile deprivation of the American baby produces an adult male who is clumsy in lovemaking and an adult female who is often interested in lovemaking more for the body contact involved than for the sexual gratification. Some women who become promiscuous do so apparently out of an urgent need to be held and cuddled—really an infant's desperate craving.

Evidence of the tactile poverty of the American culture was turned up in one of the rare naturalistic studies done on touching. Vidal Starr Clay observed the tactile behavior of mother-and-child pairs in public places. She found, as one might expect, that children are touched less and less as they grow older; however, the youngsters who had the most physical contact with their mothers were not the so-called infants-in-arms, but the toddlers—the under-two-year-olds who were able to walk. In our culture, a host of things come between mother and infant—bottles, clothing, cribs, carriages. The child enjoys a brief tactile heyday when he begins to walk, and then contact steadily diminishes, probably dropping off sharply at the age of about five or six.

Clay's observations also revealed that most of the contacts between mother and child were a matter of care-taking—wiping noses, straightening clothes—rather than an expression of affection, and that little girls were touched more often than little boys. Other studies have found that baby girls are treated to more demonstrations of affection than are boys, and that girls are generally weaned later—just as boys are indulged more with physical freedom, girls are given more emotional freedom. The American mother seems so careful not to overstimulate her sons sexually or emotionally that, in fact, she probably understimulates them. Perhaps that's one reason why grown American women are more comfortable about touching than are American men.

To the baby, to be held is to be loved. But as he matures the *way* he's held conveys more than just love; it tells him a lot about the person who is holding him. He knows when he's being handled by someone who is nervous and not used to babies. He can literally feel the tenseness that goes with anger or fear and the lethargy of depression. And at some early age he begins to absorb his mother's feelings about sex, which are also transmitted to him nonverbally. As the psychiatrist Alexander Lowen has explained, if a mother is ashamed of her body, she will convey that shame—assuming that she breast-feeds at all—in the tense and ungracious way she offers the baby her breast. If she finds genitals repulsive, she will show it as she touches the baby's genitals during diapering. It must be difficult, if not impossible, to hide such very basic reactions from the avid awareness of the infant.

Babies learn fast from all the sensory experiences offered them, though we tend to underrate their learning ability, just as we underrate that of the fetus. The psychologist Jerome Bruner believes that infants take in many more details of their environment than adults ever thought they did and that even very small babies invent theories to explain what they perceive. A baby just three weeks old will become disturbed if—through the ventriloquism of microphones—his mother's voice seems to come, not from where she stands, but from some place else. Already, he has formed a theory that links direction of sound to what he sees. Bruner maintains that babies have an innate ability to construct logical theories from scraps of evidence. Although this idea is relatively new, scientists have for years discussed other possibly innate responses. They have, for example, observed that from a very early age infants are enormously attracted to the human face and especially to the eyes. And this response to eyes is a vital part of a particular behavioral sequence that takes place early in the life of every normal individual.

At birth, a baby can distinguish light and darkness and little else; however, at about four weeks of age he learns to focus his own eyes and what occurs soon after that is perhaps the smallest but possibly one of the most important events in his life. One day, he looks straight up into his mother's eyes—and smiles. Even blind babies make a similar response at about the same age. And mothers almost invariably react with great excitement and delight. Some scientists believe that all these behaviors are innate: the eye contact, the baby's smile, and even the mother's delight. The argument runs that this delight obviously has survival value, from an evolutionary point of view, since for humans motherhood entails a lengthy, demanding, exhausting and often unrewarding period of child care. It might be crucial for the mother at this point in her child's life to feel she's getting some positive response from the baby, some payment for services rendered.

In an attempt to pin down exactly which aspects of the face babies react to and at what ages, scientists have run experiments in which they flashed specially designed cards at infants. They found that babies just two months old smile if shown a card with a pair of small, sharp dots arranged horizontally on it—in other words, a configuration like a pair of eyes—and that at that age they're more apt to respond to the dots than to a painting of a whole face. The number of dots doesn't seem to matter, nor does their shape nor the shape of the card. But as the baby grows older, the stimulus has to become more and more like the human face to interest him. It has to acquire a mouth, it has to move, and eventually, by the age of about seven months, it has to smile.

While the basic attraction to eyes *may* be inborn, it's possible to explain it without invoking innate behavior. The infant reacts favorably to any stimulus that's familiar and at the same time complex enough to interest him. At birth his range of vision is limited to eight to ten inches in front of his nose, and that's the distance at which his mother's face is presented to him during feedings and at many other times of the day. At first, the full complexity of her face may be too much for him to take in, but the eyes—bright, moving, swimming up out of the blur created by his own immature vision—catch his attention. They may, as the British psychologist Ian Vine puts it, "provide a convenient 'anchor' for subsequently greater scanning and perception of the full complexity of the face."

As the baby grows he learns not only to recognize familiar faces but to recognize expressions, and soon he becomes more skilled at reading nonverbal behavior than he will, perhaps, ever be again in his life. As Desmond Morris wrote in *The Naked Ape*:

> At the pre-verbal stages, before the massive machinery of symbolic, cultural communication has bogged us down, we rely much more on tiny movements, postural changes and tones of voice than we need to in later life. . . . If the mother is making tense and agitated movements, no matter how concealed, she will communicate these to her child. If at the same time she gives a strong smile, it does not fool the infant, it only confuses it.

The baby becomes a child and the child continues to be especially sensitive to the messages of the face. Because he hasn't learned yet not to stare into another person's face, and because he's not as distracted by words as is an adult, he is able literally to *see* excitement, fear, shame, joy. The importance children attach to the face is indicated by the drawings typically done by preschool youngsters: human figures, almost always topped by enormous and carefully detailed heads. And nine out of ten children, if touched simultaneously on hand and face and asked to say where they were touched, will indicate their faces, while only half of all normal adults name the face in the same situation. Silvan Tomkins has suggested that the prime object of dread in childhood is not angry words or an angry-sounding voice, but an angry face. He explained:

> I have treated children in whom it seemed clear that the dread of the angry, unloving, shaming face of the parent was so much greater than the dread of spanking and other punishments, that these punishments were sought by the child to reduce the dread of the disapproving and frightening face. Since the face of the parent is more loving following the discharge of aggression, some children provoked this discharge of aggression via a more harmless channel such as being sent to his room, or being spanked, so that they are spared the dreaded facial interaction. . . .

This is a novel explanation of a phenomenon long noted by psychiatrists—the child who *wants* to be punished. The usual psychiatric explanation is that he feels secretly guilty, and being punished relieves his guilt, but this doesn't mean that he may not *also* prefer a spanking to the sight of his father's or mother's angry face.

Two and three year olds are sometimes enormously frightened of masks. This may be partly a reflection of what Selma Fraiberg, a child psychoanalyst, calls "magic thinking"—the child thinks that, if the face has changed, there may be a different person behind it—but it may also reflect the fact that children depend so heavily on the faces of others for clues to their reactions. Children also sometimes develop face prejudices that can turn out to be perfectly logical reactions resulting from the fact that they see more than adults see. When my daughter was four or five, for example, she would sometimes remark of some adult or other that she "didn't like his face." It always turned out that what bothered her wasn't unattractiveness in the sense that adults use the word, but a habitual expression of anger or discontent.

It's disconcerting for a mother (or a father) to realize that she constantly communicates with her small children through nonverbal channels and often clearly conveys feelings and reactions she may not even be aware of having. The idea made me a little uneasy for a while, especially after I stumbled across some of the literature on the self-fulfilling prophecy.

Investigations into self-fulfilling prophecies began back in the nineteen thirties with a classic case—a six-year-old boy who kept running away from home. Each time he returned, his father insisted on hearing every detail of his adventures. Though he punished the boy afterward, it seemed clear that he took vicarious pleasure in his son's exploits. From the work that has been done since then on nonverbal communication, it's easy to guess how that pleasure was conveyed: by facial expressions, by the postures he assumed, and the very rhythm of his movements as he listened to his son's stories.

Struck by this very clear example, two Chicago psychiatrists went on to looking at other behavioral problems and found children who stole, children who set fires, others who were sexual deviates, and even some who committed murder—all of whom were actually acting out the subconscious desires of their parents. Any adult who has ever faced up, however briefly, to some of his own fantasies will find this a rather shattering idea. The overanxious mother also sometimes sets her child up to do the very thing she most dislikes: the mother who can't abide lying is the mother most likely to have a lying child.

However, repressed emotions and subconscious yearnings are part of the psychological make-up of every normal adult; parents have always communicated these things to their children, and most of the children have survived pretty well. In the future, studies of parent-child interaction will undoubtedly teach us much more about just how families communicate, but it will be a long time before we can teach a parent how *not* to communicate certain feelings nonverbally. And of course before one can learn not to communicate them, one must face up honestly to the fact that one has them.

When it comes to the nonverbal learning of small babies, if we take Ashley Montagu's arguments seriously (and I do), then we must conclude that our whole approach to child rearing can stand some rethinking. Parents, doctors, and hospitals need to work out a way to provide the infant with a gentler transition from the womb to the everyday world. We should also make sure, I think, before committing small babies to day-care centers, that they will be held, rocked, hugged—loved—enough. It's marvelous to offer a toddler lots of intellectual stimulation and the opportunity for early learning, as good day-care centers will; but the *non*verbal learning he does in his earliest years is perhaps even more important, and the best learning situation for this is still a good relationship with adults who both enjoy him and have time for him.

The Nonverbal Code of Childhood

17

In their studies of animals, ethologists have evolved a field technique that allows them to observe and record behavior in very fine—and objective—detail, without preconceived notions. The ethologist in the wild lives among the animals until he is accepted as a normal part of their environment; then he begins to note down sequences of behavior, watching what precedes each act and what its consequences are. On the spot or perhaps later, in computer analysis, patterns are culled from these sequences so that, for example, all the different elements that go into an attack can be described: posture, facial expression, eye behavior, sound effects, and so on. Once such a pattern has been identified and pointed out to an observer, the apparently random activities of the animals take on a new significance for him—he literally sees them differently.

For the *human* ethologists, nursery school children are excellent subjects since they're more active and much less inhibited than adults. They play together, form small cooperative bands, attack one another and beat a retreat, and all the while they communicate largely by facial expressions and gestures, rarely resorting to words.

One of the pioneering ethological studies of children was done back in 1963–64 by N. G. Blurton Jones, who spent months sitting quietly in a chair in a corner of a London nursery school, recording in a notebook in fine-grained physical detail the behavior of the children. He was able to make some intriguing comparisons between the activities of young humans and those of other young primates. He noted, for example, that some childish facial expressions are strikingly similar to the expressions other primates wear. The stare, lowered eyebrows, and slight, tense frown of the attack face are much the same in child and monkey, and the smile of the child's play face—an open-mouthed grin that nevertheless shows no teeth—is very like the "smile" of the play face of other young primates. However, Jones reported that among three- to five-year-old humans there seems to be no true equivalent of the primate dominance hierarchy, though it is possible that such hierarchies do exist among older children.

Jones noted that, just as monkeys do, children go in for rough-and-tumble play that looks very much like fighting. There are, however, signals that confirm the playful nature of the behavior, both between children and between monkeys. The child, for example, wears the play face. He laughs and jumps up and down with both feet together. He only pretends to hit. When chased, he takes turns being pursuer and pursued; and so on. Monkeys exchange similar signals.

Baby monkeys that are never given a chance to play

with others their own age grow up into lonely, unsociable creatures, much worse off, in fact, than babies deprived of their mothers but allowed to play occasionally with their peers. For infant monkeys at least, play seems to be even more important than mothering as a socializing influence, and Jones suggests that it must be vital for humans, too, since the child's nonverbal repertoire actually contains more this-is-play signals than the monkey's repertoire does.

Jones also noted that there were a few children who went in for rough-and-tumble play hardly at all. They talked often and well to anyone who would listen, they read a lot and mostly played alone. Since rough-and-tumble motor patterns and expressions appear as early as eighteen months of age and perhaps even earlier, Jones wondered whether these children had missed out on vital play experience at a critical age, and were now too old to learn it.

Nursery school children have also been studied by a team of ethologists assembled by Dr. Michael Chance in Birmingham, England, and ethological description is neatly illustrated by the team's account of how children quarrel over a toy. One child, they report, wears an angry frown—eyebrows drawn down at the inner corners—and thrusts his head and often his chin forward, holding his lips tense and also pushed forward. And he glares. He may strike the other child, using a particular blow called a beat, which is characteristic of preschoolers: arm raised, fingers curled, palm facing forward. The struck child often crouches, cries, or runs away, wearing all the while an escape expression: brows pulled down at the outside ends, mouth open and rather square, face flushed. Humans who are about to attack seldom flush—according to Desmond Morris, they're more apt to turn pale instead. Flushing is a sign of defeat.

The childish blow or beat is usually preceded by a

so-called beating posture—hand raised to head level and held there for several seconds. If the hand is held well forward and away from the head it's likely that the blow will be struck. If it's held back and close to the head, it may be simply a defensive gesture. There are, the ethologists report, a whole series of hand positions in between these extremes and the point at which the hand is poised apparently represents a point of balance between the urge to attack and the urge to escape. This is definitely a signal that can be read by the other child, since the other, when confronted by an offensive beating posture, will sometimes take to his heels even before a blow is struck, or may respond by assuming, in his turn, a defensive beating posture.

The Birmingham team paid considerable attention to the children's facial expressions. From their observations they concluded that there are six ways to frown, each involving a different pattern of eyebrow position and forehead wrinkling. There are eight ways to smile, and each smile is used in particular situations. These facial gestures are apparently carried over intact into adult life.

The common-garden smile is the upper smile, used in greetings, which reveals only the upper teeth. However, there are variations on the pattern. For example, formal introductions don't call for a show of teeth at all, just up-turned lips, while when a child runs eagerly to his mother—or when lover greets lover—the mouth may be fairly wide open though it will still be only the upper teeth that show. The upper smile becomes the lip-in smile when the teeth are sunk lightly into the lower lip. People use the lip-in smile when meeting someone they feel subordinate to. The broad smile, which displays both upper and lower teeth, occurs during pleasurable excitement and is somewhat different from the open-mouth smile, in which the mouth is ajar but the teeth are covered. Children at play use both these smiles but the open-mouthed version seems to be specific to the play face. There's even a nonsocial smile, the ethologists report. They call it the simple smile and it's the enigmatic, Mona Lisa look of self-pleasure. The lips curve upward but the mouth remains closed. The individual who smiles when he is alone probably smiles a simple smile. A cold smile is a smile that touches the mouth only. Subtle changes around the outer corners of the eyes are what supply the warmth in an expression. Even a broad smile is unconvincing if the eyes remain unaffected and if it's not accompanied by a lift of the eyebrows.

Though children carry these facial expressions into adult life, other childhood body gestures disappear or are transmuted. The beating posture, for example, is rarely seen in individuals over the age of six, though traces of it can be found in adult behavior. When a person touches chin or cheek with thumb and index finger, palm faced awkwardly outward toward another person, he's probably feeling threatened. Two of the Birmingham ethologists, Christopher Brannigan and David Humphries, have written:

> In more defensive situations the hand moves back, as in the *defensive beating posture*, but this is disguised by the palm being placed on the back of the neck. If you find yourself doing this, examine your motivation honestly— you will be feeling very defensive! In women especially, the *hand to neck* movement may be combined with a rather sophisticated hair-grooming action. Similarly, a driver making a mistake in overtaking and pulling in too quickly in front of another car often does a quick grooming movement through his hair followed by a *hand to neck* posture.

The social meanings of hand-to-head movements are sometimes easy to spot, both in adults and children, because the movement obviously serves a function: the eye cover when we don't want to see something, mouth cover when we're worried about talking, or trying to hide a smile. Less obvious gestures such as finger-combing the hair, head-scratching, nose-rubbing, or stroking the chin—or the beard if the individual is adult and bearded—seem related to care of the body surface but actually tend to occur at times when we're indecisive or ambivalent.

American kinesicists have noted that nose-rubbing often happens when a person is reacting negatively; and they point out that hair-grooming occurs in courtship situations. The British ethologists, however, relate grooming to ambivalence. They report that finger-combing the hair, for example, seems to occur at moments of precise balance, when the individual is momentarily poised in indecision. One nursery school boy was about to yank a classmate's pigtail when the teacher called to him; he passed his fingers through his hair and then left the little girl to go to the teacher. Head-scratching, on the other hand, seems to indicate frustration rather than ambivalence.

These days, human ethology is developing some refreshingly practical applications. The ethological method is being used to study the mentally ill, many of whom are unable or unwilling to talk, which makes their nonverbal behavior rather important. One British scientist, Ewan Grant, observed and recorded elements of behavior in a doctor-patient interview, ran a statistical analysis of his data, and found that he could cluster all the behavior he'd seen under five major headings: assertion, flight, relaxation, contact, and self-contact (grooming, etc.). He also recorded behavioral links between clusters. Flight, for example, was sometimes linked to contact by "look-at"—or, in other words, a person who showed signs of wanting to withdraw from a relationship might, after looking directly at the other person, begin instead to smile or display other contact behaviors.

Using Grant's analysis, Christopher Brannigan, with Kate Currie, worked with an autistic child, a little girl five years old. Like many autistic children, she never spoke and was terribly withdrawn; she would seldom voluntarily come near the scientists and as much as possible avoided looking at them. In ethological terms, she was almost entirely deficient in "contact and assertion behaviors." Brannigan and Currie decided to try to condition the child to the use of the behavioral links, approach and look-at, to see if the contact behaviors would follow. With pieces of chocolate and gentle praise as rewards, they taught her first to approach them and then to look at them, and smile. Smiling is one link between contact and assertion behaviors and once the child began to smile, she went on to angry-frown, thrust-head-forward, and beat—all assertive elements. These represented giant steps forward for this child, even though she was still without speech.

The ethological studies of children done in Britain are a fascinating beginning, though much more work needs to be done before we'll know, for example, how much nonverbal "language" a child should be in command of at any particular age. An even more interesting question has been partially answered: How do children learn the code? William Condon's work suggests that children learn because parents reward them nonverbally for making the right body movements—reward them with a smile, or perhaps by leaning forward and moving into heightened synchrony. These out-of-awareness lessons in out-of-awareness skills are almost certainly there to be seen once researchers begin to look for them.

18 | Clues to Character

As mimics have always known, a man's body movements are as personal as his signature. And as novelists have always known, they often reflect his character.

Research on human communication has often neglected the individual, yet it's obvious that most of us can sometimes do a rough character analysis on the basis of the way a man moves—rigidly, casually, vigorously—and that the way a man moves is a fairly stable personality characteristic.

Take the simple act of walking: of alternately lifting each foot, carrying it forward, and placing it on the ground. This can convey a surprising amount. The man who habitually thrusts hard with his heels as he walks strikes us as a determined individual. If he's a fast walker he may seem impatient or aggressive, though the same thrust at a slower, more even pace may come across instead as patient persistence. A person can also walk with very little thrust—as if crossing a lawn and trying not to trample the grass—and this gives an impression of tentativeness. And since the leg action begins at the hip, there are other variations. A relatively exaggerated lift of each hip seems quite jaunty; if at the same time the hips are rotated slightly the walker is casual, easygoing. Add a bit more swing, some emphasis, a slight figure-eight shaping, and you have the kind of walk that, when a woman does it, turns a man's head.

This is the "how" of body movement as opposed to the "what"—not the act of walking but how the person walks and not the act of shaking hands but how it's done; the system that has evolved for studying it is called Effort-Shape. The Effort-Shape analyst looks at the flow of movement—at tension and relaxation, strength and lightness, suddenness, directness, and so on—and at shaping, which is really a dancer's concept: at the forms the body makes in space.

Actually, Effort-Shape had its beginnings in a system of dance notation. Its history is very much the history of one remarkable man, Rudolph Laban. Originally an architect and painter, Laban turned to choreography in the early 1900s in Europe. He devised a system for notating dance—for recording the dancers' movements—called Labanotation, which has been used to record ballet, modern and folk dance for over thirty years.

With the rise of the Nazis, Laban left Central Europe for England. There, during the war, he was asked to investigate efficiency and fatigue in British industry. His approach to the problem was entirely different from the more familiar Time-Motion study approach, which concentrates on finding the shortest and quickest way to do things, treating the worker at times as if he were part of the machine. Laban tried to design movement sequences that would be comfortable, nonmonotonous, and that wouldn't overemphasize any one kind of exertion. For example, if a worker were required to lift something heavy, the shortest way to do it might be to heave it straight up. Laban would instead suggest a two-step lift, perhaps an upward swing to the right first and then one to the left, so that the momentum and the rhythm of the movement were both behind the lift.

It was through these industrial studies that Laban developed another, different system for describing and analyzing movement—Effort-Shape. In a sense, what Labanotation records is analogous to the notes and keys of music, while Effort-Shape is like music dynamics: *pianissimo, forte,* and so on. Laban found that with the same terms he could now notate, not just dance, but any interaction, even people sitting around and discussing something together. Furthermore, his system described both how a man related to the outside world (space) and how he discharged and modified his energy (effort). In demonstrating the interrelationship of these two things, he was attempting to get at the biological root of man's communication. And he was able to be both objective and exact. As one of Laban's disciples, Irmgard Bartenieff, explained, "we can describe a 'proud' posture, a 'seductive' walk, a 'demanding' gesture in terms of specific, objective movement features."

Effort-Shape has been applied to dance training and actor training, to dance therapy and physical rehabilitation, to studies in child development and research in psychotherapy, and even to cross-cultural research. In England, Warren Lamb, who helped Laban develop the Effort-Shape system, has been using it as an industrial consultant for about twenty years. Lamb evaluates applicants for management positions by analyzing their movement styles. He has already studied over five thousand individuals and in a sense his work provides a rough, practical validation for the system. Apparently, it works—though so far no experimental validation has been devised.

There's something almost uncanny about Laban's kind of movement analysis—primarily, I think, because as a result of a two-year training program, the Effort-Shape analyst sees so much more than the layman can even begin to. To get an idea of what an Effort-Shape expert sees, I went out to Bronx State Hospital to interview Martha Davis, then a staff psychologist there doing movement research while finishing her doctorate. About nine years ago Ms. Davis was working as a research assistant at the Albert Einstein Psychiatric Day Hospital when she met Irmgard Bartenieff, the woman who brought Effort-Shape to this country. First intrigued and then involved, she eventually collaborated with Mrs. Bartenieff on a series of pioneering movement analyses of group and family therapy.

Ms. Davis showed me a film of one such session. As it opened, two men, doctor and patient, entered a room and moved across in front of the camera to take seats facing it. What struck me immediately was that something was very wrong with the patient. The sound track had been turned off so there was no dialogue to provide a clue; however, he simply didn't move the way normal people move. Ms. Davis spelled out for me what was different about him. There was the way he walked: in a kind of monotone, very slowly and evenly, with little shifting of weight from one foot to the other. And there was the way he sat: with perfect symmetry, legs uncrossed, arms hanging down at his sides, never moving the trunk of his body. That degree of stillness and that kind of symmetry are typical of certain schizophrenics, Ms. Davis explained. She has found that some movement disturbances appear to be good indices of the severity of the patient's illness, and others seem to correlate with specific diagnoses.

As the film went on the patient moved very little, but

whenever he did move the effect was decidedly odd. He would turn his head from left to right with a kind of dreamlike slowness and at the end of the movement he might suddenly begin to scratch his face, raking it quickly and harshly over and over again with his nails. He would start a movement and not finish it, or he would start one and then jerk into doing something else altogether. Every motion was thwarted, his rhythm and sequences were fragmented, and it was as if that weird slowness drew a barrier between himself and others. I was reminded of something Birdwhistell had told me: With psychotic children sometimes the mother is aware from the time an infant is just a few months old that there's something terribly wrong about the way it moves.

For contrast, we looked next at the psychiatrist in the film. He sat leaning slightly forward toward the patient, and when he gestured, which wasn't often, the movement was quick, light, economical, and spatially clear. At one point the patient slumped to one side and the doctor reached out, took him by the arm and pulled him upright again. The reaching out was done with a kind of firm directness. There was nothing sudden, sharp, or wasted in the motion and when he took the patient's arm he didn't push down on it or pull over but very evenly and *clearly* drew him upright. All in all, Ms. Davis said, her reading of the doctor—an educated impression rather than a real analysis—was that he was a firm, gentle, sensitive man, a bit intellectual and aloof.

If Ms. Davis had been going on to do an in-depth analysis, she would have gone about it in one of two ways: she could have looked for and recorded in detail the phrases of movement—the sequences—that seemed characteristic for each man; or she might instead have gone over and over the film, checking it each time for what are called Effort-Shape parameters. These parameters are numerous and complex, but briefly and in simplified form, here are some of the features she would have been looking for:

The gesture-posture ratio is a way to tell how involved in the situation the individual is. It distinguishes two kinds of movements: the gestural, in which the individual uses only a part of his body, and the postural, which spreads throughout the body and usually entails a weight shift as well. Postural movement literally has more weight behind it and can be used as a measure of involvement. A man waving his arms wildly in anger will appear unconvincing if the movement is limited to arm gestures and never spreads to the rest of his body. A postural shift, Ms. Davis cautioned, isn't just a matter of shifting the weight of the trunk of the body—unless other body parts are involved, this shifting is called a gesture of the trunk. Even walking can be gestural and consequently a sign of withdrawal, as it was with the patient in the film. But it's the ratio of postural to gestural movements that counts, rather than the sheer number of postural movements. A man can sit very still, listening, but if, when he does move, the motion spreads to involve his whole body, he will seem very attentive—much more so than someone who does a lot of moving, perhaps constantly fidgeting with one body part or another.

Body attitude reflects the persistent attitudes and orientations of the individual. One can hold oneself narrowly, or actively sit forward, or sink into oneself, and so on, and these postures—and their variety or lack of it—literally embody the way one relates and orients himself to others.

Effort flow refers to the range of movement from tense to relaxed, from controlled to uncontrolled, or in technical terms, from bound to free. When a person threads a needle, or carries a hot cup of coffee, his movements are bound; when he makes sweeping arm gestures they're free. Some people vary their effort flow a lot—children do. In adults such lively effort flow is related to characteristics like spontaneity and flexibility. At the other end of the spectrum, mental patients and the very old or sick sometimes move in a monotone as the patient in the film did. Movements can be light or strong, direct or indirect, sudden or sustained—or they may not be noticeably any of these things. In general, effort is thought to be related to mood or feeling—a strong downward motion is usually assertive, while light, free touching reflects gentleness or sensitivity. Or think of the bound slowness of a funeral procession, the strong, quick, aggressive quality of a war dance, or the rhythmic, indirect, free flow through the body that expresses sexuality in dance.

Shape flow and *shaping* refer to the way the body uses space. The trick to seeing this seems to be to try to think of ordinary movements as if it were ballet, so that one can sense the body literally sculpting itself in space. The body can be seen extending into three dimensions: narrowing or widening, rising or sinking, advancing or retreating. People sometimes concentrate their movements in one plane or another. A person moving mainly in the horizontal plane appears to be very spread out: his elbows project and he takes up more than his share of space on a sofa. A person who moves mostly in the vertical plane looks as though he carries himself within a picture frame: he walks with short steps, draws himself up tall to shake hands, and when he sits he lowers himself with both hands on the chair arms, while square-ly facing front. The individual who favors the sagital plane strides along with knees and ankles close together and sits by moving straight back into a chair or pulling it forward under him. In conversation he often seems to be coming right at you. Interpretations of these movement styles are suggested in their descriptions—though, of course, not many people fit so neatly into one category or another.

These main shape dimensions relate both to temperament and to the individual's reaction to a situation. In general, a man's style reflects how he copes with his own inner feelings and how he adapts to outer realities. Especially important are the variety and complexity both of his effort elements and of his use of space, because these are the chief clues to his ability to cope—and to be flexible rather than rigid in his dealings with others. The importance of such flexibility was dramatically demonstrated in a filmed group therapy session analyzed by Ms. Davis and Mrs. Bartenieff. There was a striking contrast in the movement styles of two members of the group. One of them, Carol, said very little but her movements were complex and they varied in intensity. Another woman, Diane, talked loudly and often and, if one didn't look at the way she moved, she might have seemed the most active and involved member of the group. But her gestures were limp and repetitive and she made very few postural shifts. In spite of her talkativeness, she was withdrawn and cut off from her own feelings. A confrontation between Carol and Diane toward the end of the session demonstrated that, even on a verbal level, Diane couldn't really be reached while Carol was very much *there*—responsive and involved.

All this sounds deceptively simple, but in actual fact it's enormously hard to *see* in Effort-Shape terms unless someone's movements are broken down and explained to you. To give readers a chance to try to see for themselves, I asked Ms. Davis to do movement analyses of two television personalities. She spent several hours observing first David Frost and then Dick Cavett, two talk-show hosts seen coast to coast. With the sound switched off Ms. Davis made notes—not as systematically as she would have for a research project, but according to what struck her as some salient characteristics of each man.

"These are impressions," she told me, "backed up

with technical descriptions, but they're not meant to be a really detailed analysis."

Here is what she saw and recorded:

David Frost usually sits slouched on the edge or side of a chair, facing his guest, head forward, with knitted brow or pleasant smile, his eyes in clear, sustained contact as he listens. His movement varies considerably in the body part used, the size and direction of the movement and the spatial planes used. Transitions from one direction to another are often angular and abrupt and sometimes there are small, erratic fluctuations in direction within a long sequence, which give an impression of awkwardness or uneasiness.

Frost's movement is rarely sinuous, slow, light, or successive. The principal kinds of intensity and accent are quickness, strength, and directness, whether in the small, sharp, angular movements of his head as he announces a station break or in his long, varied gesticulations punctuated with quick changes and forceful jabs. In Frost's movement the effort flow—continuous variations between bound flow and free—varies a great deal within a gesture and depending on whom he is with. At times he may limit his movement to bound fidgeting or to small, repetitive, and controlled pushes of the forearm while speaking. At other times he may gesticulate with free swings and sweeps of the arm.

A number of adjectives come to mind in describing his movement style: spontaneous, varied, driving, sometimes awkward or erratic, quick to respond, unpretentious, informal, and emotionally involved. Frost can look quite different from evening to evening, and in three viewings the degree to which his movement varied from guest to guest was dramatic. This, I think, supports the impression that, although he is obviously in control of the show and constantly alert to how the interviews appear, he is also genuinely, emotionally involved in the dialogues.

Dick Cavett has a very different movement style. He sits upright, open and slightly back, and so is oriented to guest, audience and camera all at once. His movement is very clear, precise and "clean," i.e., there is more stress on spatial aspects than on intensity or effort qualities, and the effort flow is usually even and controlled, the directions always distinct. For example, from an actively held, very upright position he will gesture bilaterally with a quick, crisp start, the movement becoming even and direct in a large spatial pattern, and continuing precise to the end. At the same time, his trunk may shift as a unit, without twisting or bending at the waist.

Cavett has directness and quickness and some strength and lightness, but these dynamics appear sparingly and he has less variation than Frost—in body parts used, in sequence of directions, as well as in what he actually does. Cavett does not vary in movement nearly so much from guest to guest as Frost does, but like Frost he is very quick to respond and very sensitive to his guests. He sometimes picks up not only the gesture of a guest but its quality as well. The impression conveyed by his movement is one of formality, shyness yet command, sensitivity, control of personal feelings and a keen alertness and stress on intellectual understanding.

As I read this analysis I realized that I had sensed the occasional awkwardness of Frost, and his very real involvement, as well as the sensitivity and control of Cavett—though I couldn't have begun to say where my impressions came from.

Effort-Shape is still so new in this country that only a handful of people are trained in it and they all know one another. Foremost is Irmgard Bartenieff, who originally studied dance under Rudolph Laban in Germany when she was in her early twenties. She came to the United States in 1937, but during the fifties made frequent trips to Europe to consult with Laban and Warren Lamb during the period when Effort-Shape theory was crystallizing.

Mrs. Bartenieff is the kind of person legends grow up around. Tiny, sixtyish, with a lithe, trim dancer's body that a nineteen-year-old might envy, she is almost uncanny in her ability to read body movement. She first made a real impression on the psychiatrists at Albert Einstein College of Medicine one day when a group of them were watching a family therapy session together through a one-way-vision screen. The sound system broke down, and so the doctors all filed out to go into conference to discuss the session. Mrs. Bartenieff stayed on to observe. When she at last joined the conference, someone thought to ask what she'd seen. She provided a whole read-out on what had been going on that both amazed and impressed the group.

"The incident I'll always remember, though," Ms. Davis recalled, "was something that happened while I was training with her. We were behind the one-way screen one day and the sound broke down. We were watching a regular group therapy session and a new young woman came in, very well put together, very vivacious, and she started talking right away. For about fifteen minutes I watched and I got very frustrated. There was something strange about the woman's movement pattern but I couldn't put my finger on it—it almost seemed as if we didn't have the terms to describe it. And all the time Irmgard was writing away, and after a while she said, half to herself:

"'Very interesting. I've never seen anything like this before. This woman is very depressed.'

"And I said:

"'Depressed? She's a dynamo.'

"'Oh, no. She's suicidal.'

"A few minutes later the sound came on and we

listened. And there was the woman talking about poisoning herself. It was really a spooky experience."

Later, Mrs. Bartenieff explained what it was that was so peculiar about the way the woman moved: She would begin a movement with lightning speed—which in itself is unusual—and then it would become suddenly bound and direct. In a sense, it was as if the movement impulse were strangled, as if she were killing her own impulse. The pattern is very rare—Ms. Davis has never seen anything like it since. She recalls that nurses on the ward used to complain about how uncomfortable they felt when they were around this strangely vivacious patient, though they could never say what it was about her that bothered them.

Mrs. Bartenieff now heads the Effort-Shape program at the Dance Notation Bureau in New York, an organization founded some thirty years ago for the purpose of developing and teaching Labanotation and of preserving dance scores. Students, who come there now also to study Effort-Shape, include dancers and dance therapists, anthropologists, and the occasional psychologist or psychiatrist. But Effort-Shape grew out of dance, and it is through the study of dance that Effort-Shape is making some of its most interesting contributions to anthropology and psychology. For the past four or five years Mrs. Bartenieff has been involved in choreometrics—an anthropological analysis of folk-dance styles the world over, part of a project conceived and headed by a folk-music expert, Alan Lomax. Mrs. Bartenieff and an Effort-Shape colleague, Forrestine Paulay, had planned to use the Laban system to analyze filmed folk dances of different cultures. However, Effort-Shape was designed to record individual variations in movement style, and the two researchers found that the broader, cultural differences were obscured by a mass of detail; so with Lomax they experimented and produced a new recording system—called choreometrics—that was based on Effort-Shape but could be used on the cultural level to code dance and movement style.

People have always been aware of cultural differences in body movement. To anyone who has seen films of both, it's obvious that the Eskimo with his squared-off, straddled stance and his energetic, angular movements is completely different from the Samoan, who may walk or dance with an undulating, wavelike movement that spreads from the waist, and gesture with sinuous, curved motions in which hands, forearms, upper arms, and shoulders all have a part. But with choreometrics it's possible to replace such general impressions with objective descriptions of observable movement features.

What the choreometrics researchers discovered was that in each culture there was a strong relationship between dance style and the commonest everyday movements. The movements that came to be echoed in dance were the ones that were so familiar, so acceptable, or so important to the community that all took pleasure in watching or repeating them. Among the Eskimos, for example, the greatest hunters, one after another, will dance before the assembled group. Standing straddled with a drum in the left hand, drumstick in the right, they bring the stick down and diagonally across the body to strike the drum. In seal hunting or salmon fishing, the Eskimo uses the same sturdy posture and thrusts his spear or harpoon down and across his body in a very similar action.

After analyzing many films, the research team found that it was actually possible to divide the world into two parts: one consisting of all the cultures in which the torso is moved as a compact, one-unit system, the other of all those in which it is articulated as several units, with easy twists and undulations from the waist. Think of the emphatic thrusting dances of the American Indian as opposed to the sinuousness of the belly dance or the Hawaiian hula, to take three of the more dramatic examples. The one-unit body attitude dominates the Amerindian and Eurasian worlds; the multiunit attitude centers in Africa with extensions through India and Polynesia.

In *Folk Song, Style and Culture*, the Lomax team wrote of the undulating, sinuous character of African dance and gesture that it "mimes, recalls, and reinforces the sexual act, especially the woman's part in it. Thus a constant current of pleasurable, erotic feeling runs openly through much of African life, warming it like sunlight."

The book points out that in Africa life always depended on a high birthrate, on large families, large agricultural labor gangs that included women, and on polygamy. To the American Indian, a high birthrate would simply have meant more mouths to feed so "the feminine, the pelvic, the fertile" was not part of his movement repertoire.

Effort-Shape has had some interesting effects on the study of child development. Before Mrs. Bartenieff became involved in choreometrics, she worked with Dr. Judith Kestenberg, a child psychiatrist, on movement analysis of newborn babies. Observing twenty infants over the first five days of life, they found that each already had its own style of movement, reflected in patterns of effort and shape flow. This is what the layman observes when he notices that some babies are more active, while others seem softer and vaguer, and so on.

Dr. Kestenberg was trained by Warren Lamb and Marion North in England and by Mrs. Bartenieff during years of mutual exchange. Her special interest is children; she has done developmental studies of youngsters from birth to eleven years of age and has evidence that individual effort-flow patterns are genetic, related to temperament, and that they remain fairly constant over the years. She has developed a way of plotting the continuous changes of effort flow on a curve, and she believes that, as a child develops, a different kind of rhythm predominates in his movement as he passes through each of Freud's psychosexual stages of development—oral, anal, phallic, and genital—rhythms that can be read from the effort-flow curves.

In terms of psychoanalytic theory, however, Effort-Shape is perhaps less closely related to the work of Freud than it is to that of Willhelm Reich and, more recently, Alexander Lowen, for these two men recognized that psychological problems are often reflected in physical characteristics. Reich, noting facial expressions, areas of body tension, and patterns of fidgeting, saw them all as ways of dealing with emotions, a part of the patient's "character armor"—constant tension in the neck might develop from a fear of being attacked from behind; tension in the mouth, throat and neck could come from a determination not to weep; a stiffly-held pelvis might have started as a way to deaden sexual sensations. Reich, and later Lowen, concentrated on areas of tension in the body and on ways to treat them and the psychological problems that went with them. Though Effort-Shape makes no psychological inferences from what it analyzes, on the other hand it also describes both movement and rigidity.

Effort-Shape is finally being recognized now by kinesicists, with whom Martha Davis has done work comparing methods and interpretations. Because the focus of each discipline is so different—one on individual movement flow, the other on general nonverbal vocabulary—the contrast has been interesting. When Ms. Davis and the kinesicists look at a film together, she sees much more constancy. She is recording a style, a recurrent way of acting and reacting, while the kinesicist records recurring gestures that serve as signals in the interaction.

On one occasion, Ms. Davis joined Albert Scheflen and others to look at a film of a family therapy session. Several times, Scheflen pointed out courting behaviors—palming and so on—on the part of one woman in the film. But to Ms. Davis there was nothing seductive about the quality of her movement: it was tense, bound, angular, almost tortured. The therapist who had been filmed with the family happened to be there at the screening that day, and he confirmed that he had experienced the woman as tense and controlled rather than seductive. It seemed clear that, just as a man can modify the meaning of the words "I love you" by the tone of voice in which he utters them, so in this film the impact of what the woman did—her courting behavior—was modified by how she did it—by the quality of her movements.

I asked Ms. Davis if she thought it would be possible to fake movement quality. Warren Lamb, for example, has noted that a movement appears contrived and unspontaneous if it's gestural rather than postural. When a public speaker moves his hands neatly in conventional, rehearsed gestures, putting nothing else of his body into it, he comes across as unspontaneous, unconvincing, and probably uninteresting; so I had wondered if one could learn to control movement quality. But apparently it's so complex, and so many fine shades of change are expressed throughout the body, that Ms. Davis believes a false image would be impossible to orchestrate.

"It would be like the centipede's problem," she said. "You know: if he were ever to start thinking about which leg to move next, he'd become paralyzed."

19 | Public Order

When a man walks down most public streets in daylight, he takes it for granted that nobody will assault him or bar his way. In a casual conversation, he usually assumes that the person he's talking to won't insult him, lie to him, try to order him around, or in general create a scene. Through their nonverbal behavior people signal to one another that they can be trusted, just as, among apes and monkeys, one animal signals to another that it means no harm. Yet threatening possibilities are always there, since we're eternally dependent on the good behavior of others. Reading Erving Goffman, one gets a sense of just how vulnerable human beings are.

Goffman, a professor of sociology at the University of Pennsylvania, is very often the starting point for communication research. In a sense, he supplies the framework and others fill in the behavioral details, for although he is himself a shrewd observer of the small behaviors, he goes beyond that—concerning himself with the conscious and unconscious assumptions on which all of us base our everyday lives.

Goffman doesn't have a laboratory. Instead, he has a filing system. When he writes, he puts together things he has read, bits of novels, newspaper clippings, items from books of etiquette, and what he learned in a year he spent studying the social structure of a mental institution. To this he adds his own systematic observations made in social situations, from cocktail parties to public meetings. The results, in cool, precise, measured prose, are his books on face-to-face interaction.

In recent years, Professor Goffman has turned his attention more and more to public order, a field of study that has undeniable importance in an era when order is so often disrupted. In the past, social scientists considered it from quite a different perspective, concentrating on the breakdown of order, and consequently there's a considerable literature on riots and other collective outbursts. Goffman's approach is to look instead at normal behavior, to analyze the rules that ordinarily apply.

He has observed that the dealings men routinely have with one another universally seem to develop their own ground rules. There are rules for maneuvering on a crowded sidewalk; for where to stand in a sparsely populated elevator; for the circumstances in which it's all right to address a remark to a stranger. Because, ordinarily, there is little to be gained by trickery or by defying the rules, people trust one another to the point where much of the time the rules are really just semiconscious assumptions. It becomes easier to understand why people become so anxious about certain public transgressions if we look first at what some of these assumptions are.

Take the matter of dress, for example, which is clearly a matter of personal choice. Dressing as we're expected to dress is one way of expressing respect for the social situation and the people present at it. Dress can alienate or it can persuade. Out on the West Coast, half a dozen psychology students went shop-lifting to investigate that point. As long as they were well dressed—in suits and ties—other customers either failed to notice their pilferage or looked the other way. When they dressed as hippies instead, they were watched suspiciously wherever they went.

Men have always used their clothing and appearance to signal who they are. In the past, a man's dress expressed his status, his position in the social hierarchy, while for a woman it doubled as a seductive ploy. Hippies have used the same idiom to signal their refusal to play the status game. Their dress reflected both what they were and what they were not: it simultaneously served as a mutual-recognition signal and as a subtle dig at the society they rejected. Taking dress, which is one behavior available for portraying respect for an occasion, they have used it to portray disrespect. What Goffman has called "the revolutionaries of decorum" use the same basic idiom as the most uptight social climbers do, but they use it in their own, inverted, Alice-in-Wonderland way.

Just as hippies invert some of the rules of order, radicals upend others.

"What happens in confrontation politics," writes Goffman, "is that persons in each other's presence decline intentionally to sustain one or more of the fundamental rules or order. Mental patients use the same strategies for different reasons."

Goffman often uses his knowledge of mental patients to hold up a kind of mirror to the normal world. In the transgressions of the mentally ill, we can see just what it is that we ordinarily expect of one another. Mental symptoms often signal that the person is not prepared to keep to his place. As Goffman explained it:

> In a hospital setting, patients will in a conversation put to you a question much more candid, delicate and probing than would anyone but your analyst. They will, when you address them, not answer back. They will be exquisitely slovenly in their dress or withdrawn in their manner or when you're talking will come and lean into the conversation or interrupt it physically. These are all devices aimed at the rules of order.

Radical groups—black, student, or feminist—have similarly attacked the rules of order—and signified their refusal to know their "place"—when they have occupied a building, seized the microphone at a public meeting, addressed a dean or politician by his first name, or used even more mundane—and ingenious—techniques.

Such confrontations have become common in recent years even in the once-sacrosanct confines of the courtroom. Dwight Macdonald in his introduction to *The Tales of Hoffman*—an edited transcript of the trial of the Chicago Seven—pointed out that when the Wobblies were brought to trial back in 1918, they accepted the usual courtroom conventions and behaved as if they shared the values and life-style of the court, even though they were all anarchists "as bold and ingenious in anti-establishment disruption outside the courtroom as their lineal descendants, Tom Hayden's SDS and Abbie Hoffman's Yippies. . . . " The Wobblies had no civic illusions, but like most radicals until the recent crop, they separated their public style of behavior from their personal one. By contrast, the defendants in the Chicago trial constantly and unpredictably challenged the court: they talked back; their lawyers made an issue out of when and where they might go to the bathroom; they asked permission to present Bobby Seale with a birthday cake in court; and Abbie Hoffman and Jerry Rubin even arrived one day got up in judicial robes. In general, they refused to behave, as expected to, in an orderly way.

Most defendants, however, ordinarily behave with patient sobriety, cooperating politely with the system that proposes to punish them. A power structure almost always rests on a kind of collusion: the subordinate accepts certain limitations, certain rules that he actually has the power to overturn. What appears to have happened now is that radical groups have realized the degree to which they themselves have been sustaining the power structure. However, Goffman cautions that:

"We're not talking about the breakdown of public order; we're just talking about a strategic device and it may on some level be more explicable in terms of the analysis of life you could draw out of Emily Post than it is from anything you could find in Lenin or Marx. During the Depression we had a lot of very revolutionary, fundamentally alienated reaction against the establishment, I think in some respects much more profound than the current reaction, but so far as I know it never took the present form. You could shoot someone during a strike and still do it without breaking certain kinds of ground rules, for example those of dress and gender appearance.

"It may be that society has not changed profoundly. It might be just on the surface. But we *have* learned that what we thought was an absolute essential for order isn't all that essential. People are surviving."

One of the more obvious problems of public order is territoriality. Goffman has recently explored "territories of the self," which includes more than just Edward Hall's concept of the personal-space bubble. The territories that particularly interest Goffman are egocentric: wherever a man goes, he takes them with him. They include certain rights he assumes he has, such as the right not to be touched, and not to be dragged into a stranger's conversation, and the right to informational privacy—which partly refers to the questions one doesn't expect to be asked. The average American, for example, would be insulted if a casual acquaintance inquired how much money he made, though in some cultures this is considered a perfectly polite question to ask, or what his sex life was like. He would be angry if someone tried to read his mail or go through his wallet or to dig too deeply into his personal background. His need for informational privacy even extends to his appearance and the details of his behavior, for he also feels he has a right not to be stared at.

As always where there are rules of order, there are ways of breaking them, of intruding: by physical invasion of the other's space, by touching what one has no "right" to touch, by staring, by making more noise than the occasion warrants, by making uncalled-for remarks—for example, the remarks of a subordinate who speaks out of turn, or a stranger who breaks into a private conversation, or a panhandler who approaches a passerby on the street. And by defilement. In middle-class American culture, many things are potentially defiling, such as body odors and body heat—Americans hate to sit down on a chair warmed up by another or to put on a borrowed coat and find the lining still lukewarm. Anything excreted by another's body is also considered defiling, from spit to sweat and urine. Such excretions are, of course, said to carry germs; however, this may be simply a rationalization for an illogical concern about taking alien substances into the body. Certainly, our feelings about our *own* excretions are hardly logical. As Gordon Allport once pointed out, we feel that it's one thing for a man to swallow the saliva in his mouth, but quite another if he spits it into a glass and then drinks it.

Or imagine the difference between sucking blood from a small cut on your finger, and sucking it from a bandage over the cut. Bodily excretions, once they've left the body, become alien and contaminating, even to the person who originally excreted them.

Not only are there ways in which one man can intrude on another in public, but there are ways in which he can intrude on himself, by self-exposure or by making himself too available. The man whose fly is unzipped, the woman who sits with legs sprawled apart, the drunk, the person who cries in front of strangers or who confides too much—all are guilty of self-intrusions that are at least as uncomfortable to observe as to perpetrate.

Events are always arising in public life that give the impression that some intrusion has occurred, and there's a considerable amount of daily ritual that has to be gone through to nullify these impressions. When we bump into someone, we apologize; caught staring, we hastily look away. In cases of self-intrusion, the onlooker is expected to play his part. One is not supposed to notice when another person picks his nose or comes unzipped. And if forced to overhear someone else's conversation, one is expected to behave as though deaf. It's often quite easy in public to eavesdrop on a conversation, but when people do, they invariably try to conceal the fact that they're listening. Imagine what would happen if the listener candidly directed his attention to the conversation and joined in.

There's one situation in which the territories of the self are deliberately and systematically invaded—during encounter groups. Encounter participants are urged to stare at each other, to touch one another, to ask—and answer—intimate questions and to share their honest emotions, particularly the socially unacceptable ones. Most of these behaviors are taken for granted between lovers and even, up to a point, between good friends. But in an encounter group, it's strangers who share the trappings of intimacy, apparently in the hope that deeply emotional, even if temporary, relationships will result.

That we all have a mask—a face—that we present to the world is a point Goffman made in a book called *Interaction Ritual.* And we try hard to save face when necessary, to preserve the impression that we're capable and strong and to avoid looking foolish. We're concerned not only about preserving our own public image but also about those of other people. This means that the role chosen by each member of a group is usually accepted by the other members. If, for example, a man and his ex-wife turn up unexpectedly at the same party and decide to pretend that theirs was a civilized parting— though it wasn't—bystanders will, with great relief, cooperate in the charade. For if one person commits a *faux pas*, everyone's equilibrium is simultaneously threatened and must be restored.

People often cooperate in mutual face-saving in intricate and subtle ways and this kind of face-saving is at its most fascinating when it comes to one-to-one relationships. Goffman has observed that in the beginning of any friendship, particularly a male-female one, both individuals are supposed to demonstrate that they're not too readily available. At the same time, they have to get on with developing the relationship and so all this must be managed by signs, and not too obvious ones at that. These signs tip the other person off to what's likely to happen so that, as a by-product, he can save a little face himself if necessary. Especially in courtship, the individual doesn't want to be put in a position where he's openly rejected or has to do such rejecting himself.

In these circumstances, the "process of gestural hinting" can take on a lot of significance. For example, if a man tries to hold a woman's hand, she may briefly allow it; but if she doesn't want to encourage him, she will keep her own hand absolutely inert within his, will pay no attention at all to the fact that he has hold of it—in fact, she will probably immediately take up some fairly intellectual topic of conversation—and at the first opportunity she will casually disengage her hand to reach for something or to straighten her hair or whatever. And the man—most men—will get the message. And so an advance has been made and firmly rejected, and yet not a word has been said on the subject.

Goffman has pointed out that hand-holding in public in our culture, except where small children are involved, is a very specific signal, almost always a sign of sexual attraction. From adolescence on, we hold hands only with someone of the opposite sex and only when sexual attraction is at least a dormant possibility. By this small gesture, then, each person confides a part of himself to the other and simultaneously demonstrates to anyone who cares to look that he has done so. Thus, a pair of homosexuals can openly defy the world simply by joining hands in public. But the sexual connotation also sets limitations on the usefulness of the behavior. It means, for example, that two men trying to stay together while moving through a dense crowd can't do the obvious thing and simply join hands to keep from being separated.

In other public situations, also, male and female actions are shaped by the expectations of society. We define males as people chronically and almost obligatorily interested in young females and expect them to provide signs of that interest; females, though they're permitted to read those signs, are supposed to respond negatively.

An obvious illustration is the familiar street scene— man whistles at passing woman. The woman can react to this in a number of ways. She can ignore the man; she can turn and make some friendly or angry comment; or she can smile but at the same time look straight ahead and keep on walking. This last represents a kind of collusion, a breach of communication barriers, but a small one as long as she does keep on walking. But if she stops, turns, and smiles, the man may be somewhat disconcerted, for he's now obliged to make some further move or feel a fool. I've known young feminists who dislike being whistled at who have adopted this tactic—with an element of irony in posture or facial expression—and report that it works beautifully as a put-down.

Sometimes when a situation shows us up in a bad light, to save face we go about providing a correction for it in words or gestures. When the situation is minor and occurs in public, so that it's not really possible to address an explanation directly to any of the strangers present, we're more likely to use a broad, self-conscious gesture, what Goffman calls "body gloss."

For example, a man leafing through a girlie magazine in a store may take care to flip the pages fairly rapidly, so that anyone watching will assume he's simply looking for a particular article. A man who finds an abandoned parcel occupying a chair he'd like to sit in will show that he *is* merely moving it and has no designs on it by handling it by the edges in a gingerly fashion. A man who blunders into a supposedly empty room only to find a meeting in progress is apt to screw up his face and contract his upper body as he quietly withdraws and eases the door shut behind him; as Goffman says, he manages "to tiptoe with his face and upper trunk." And if a man is leaning against a wall, taking up sidewalk space, and another person approaches, the leaner is very likely to do a "loller's tuck"—however subtly, he will pull himself in and back as the other draws abreast of him, as if to make room or at any rate to indicate the will to make room.

The point demonstrated by all this is that no one is ever really alone and anonymous in a crowd; nor is he simply moving mechanically from place to place. Whenever he's out in public, he constantly and half-deliberately behaves so as to provide evidence that he is of good character. Though he may seem totally indifferent to those around him, they are, potentially, the audience, and he the actor, if a situation arises that seems to compromise him.

Making Conversation 20

Language, above all else, is what sets man apart from the other animals. Without it, culture, history—most of the things that make him what he is—would be impossible. But in face-to-face conversation language occurs within a nonverbal framework that's inextricably part of the message. That it's an important part should be obvious by now; some scientists have suggested that without the nonverbal elements, the exchange of verbal messages might be impossible.

That seems a far-out statement to make in this age of telephones and teaching machines. Certainly it is possible to exchange information with someone you can't see: to make appointments over the telephone, for example, and to pass on news and accomplish many other things. But such communication is severely limited. A brief consideration of the part nonverbal behavior plays in conversation should make that clear, and help the reader see how some of the different communication elements fit together.

Any face-to-face relationship except perhaps the most fleeting tends to seek its own equilibrium. Matters such as the relative status of the participants, how intimate they're going to be, what roles they're going to play, and what topics are suitable for discussion, are sorted out until there is some kind of shared unspoken agreement. Most often, the sorting out is done even before the individuals come together, so that when they meet they already know where they stand—if a man runs into his brother-in-law on the street, it's usually unnecessary for them to renegotiate their relationship. The kind of conversation a woman has with the postman is unlike the kind she has with her mother, and in each case the situation—the roles each will play—is pretty well predefined.

However, sometimes a new equilibrium is arrived at through subtle, nonverbal negotiations that take place during the first seconds of the encounter. Ray Birdwhistell believes that in most instances the first fifteen to forty-five seconds are predictive: that is, they are either a statement of a relationship already established, or a negotiation, and a scientist who analyzes them can use his analysis to predict how the participants will relate to one another throughout the rest of this particular encounter. Sometimes there's a recalibration of the relationship later on, but that's fairly uncommon.

One of the most important matters negotiated in those first seconds is relative status. Social scientists who know what to look for can sometimes tell quite easily who's dominant in a group. The alpha individual—to borrow the ethological term for the pack leader—talks more and in a more decisive manner and is more apt to interrupt. He is looked at more by the others, and his gestures are usually lively and vigorous. In dominance negotiations, he will probably assume a relaxed posture with raised head and unsmiling facial expression; others may signal submissiveness with lowered heads and nervous, appeasing smiles. Alpha may also try to stare another person down; in general, he has more eye room and probably also a larger personal-space bubble.

The most effective way to assert dominance is non-verbally. Scientists have demonstrated this in an experiment using video tapes. To begin with, they video-taped people reading three different messages. The content of the first was authoritarian; the second was apologetic; the third was neutral. The manner in which each message was delivered was also systematically varied: nonverbal behavior was either dominant, submissive, or neutral. When judges were brought in and asked to rate each tape on a scale from inferior to superior, from friendly to hostile, it was found that the way the message was delivered, the nonverbal variable, had a greater impact on the ratings than the verbal content did. In fact, when the message was delivered in the dominant style, its verbal content was almost irrelevant.

At the same time that dominance is being negotiated or simply reaffirmed, a mutually agreeable intimacy level is established. It's affected, of course, by status—the mailroom clerk is unlikely to be on intimate terms with the executive vice-president—and also by whether the people involved like one another or not. The behaviors used to express or negotiate intimacy are the ones by which one person tells another whether or not he likes him. This is seldom done verbally. Two people express the fact that they like each other by sharing postures; by standing close; by facing one another squarely; by looking at each other a lot and wearing an interested or pleased expression when they do so; by moving in heightened synchrony; by leaning toward one another;

by touching; and by voice quality. Some of these are also ways in which a person signals that he's paying attention. What makes them instead a statement of intimacy is a matter of degree and of the context in which they occur. Except during torrid love affairs, the whole battery of intimacy signals is seldom brought to bear all at once. Two British psychologists, Michael Argyle and J. Dean have suggested that there is a kind of intimacy equation, where the intimacy level equals the function of all these behaviors—proximity, eye contact, smiling, personal topics of conversation, etc.—taken together. If you vary one of the behaviors, you need compensating changes in the others to maintain the same level. If, for example, people who are non-intimates are to remain comfortable while standing close together, eye contact must usually be avoided and perhaps smiling as well. This is one reason why it's impossible to say that any behavior has a single, inevitable meaning. Standing close can signal a number of things and its significance can be qualified or even contradicted by other body behaviors. To decode it, you have to look at the whole equation.

Emotions are also largely conveyed and shared—if not negotiated—nonverbally. In the limpness of his gestures and his posture one man reveals his despondency; by his extreme body tension another betrays fear. Theoretically, emotional equilibrium isn't absolutely necessary to a relationship; however, conversation does become rather difficult without it. Try to imagine an encounter between a man who's grieving and another who has just won a huge lottery prize and you'll see what I mean. Emotions are contagious and given just a little time each participant begins to absorb a bit of the emotional coloration of the other.

Nonverbal signals also establish roles. We treat others differently according to their sex, age, and social class; we also behave as is appropriate to our own roles.

Some people role-play obsessively, and never vary their behavior no matter what the situation. There are women who are chronically flirtatious. Or, to use examples suggested by Ray Birdwhistell, there is the doctor at a party who insists on playing doctor at a party: by the way he carries himself, by the way he moves in and occupies your space, he almost insists that you ask what he does—and if you don't he'll tell you anyway. Or there's the favorite schoolteacher you revisit only to find that she doesn't know how to stop being a schoolteacher. She talks a little too precisely, she carries herself a little too high.

And of course people also make nonverbal statements about their maleness or femaleness, gender statements that can be part of a negotiation (for example, over whether a relationship is to be a sexual one), and others that simply reflect basic assumptions our society makes about men and women. The differences between male body language and female are pervasive and fascinating. Women in our culture tend to stand closer together, to touch the other person more, to look directly at the other more often and with longer glances, to react positively to close quarters, to mesh body rhythms more closely, and so on. Their nonverbal behavior in general reflects the fact that they're more open to personal relationships and value them more. Of course, sex roles are becoming less rigidly defined now and it's possible that in the future the body-code differences between the sexes will be less striking.

I've gone over only a few of the many ways in which humans communicate nonverbally when face to face. If you stop to think how much goes on outside the range of normal, verbal conversation, it may seem strange that humans are so preoccupied with what's said. The nonhuman primates apparently have no difficulty signaling to one another their intentions and emotions: they do it with

facial expressions, postures, gestures, and with characteristic cries. Michael Argyle has suggested that language
is unnecessary for conveying attitudes and emotions, and
must have developed for other purposes, probably as a
way to communicate about distant events and absent
objects. It has, of course, been extended to deal with
more immediate events, but Argyle suggests that it's a
relatively ineffective way to do so.

Of course, communication isn't as simple as sending
information through the verbal channel and emotions
through the nonverbal ones. On the verbal level, emotions can be precisely defined and dealt with. Because we
not only signal emotions without being aware that we're
doing it, but also receive the emotion signals of others
without being conscious of what we're reacting to,
there's a great deal of room for misunderstanding: for
deciding that the other person is angry when he's not; for
conveying disapproval yourself without intending to—
and for not conveying it clearly when you do intend
to—and so on.

There are also some nonverbal signals, such as the
markers and the stress system discovered by Birdwhistell, that are tied into verbal content and would be
meaningless without it. And still other nonverbal cues
exist solely to regulate the verbal exchange, the way
traffic signals regulate the flow of traffic. In ordinary
conversation they're indispensable. Before two people
can talk both must signal that they're paying attention.
They must stand reasonably close together, aim their
bodies and/or their heads at one another, and exchange
glances from time to time. Each also needs nonverbal
feedback from the other whenever he himself is speaking: a fairly steady gaze and certain behaviors in the
"back channel"—occasional head nods, appropriate facial reactions, and perhaps murmurs of encouragement
such as "m-hm" and "yeah." In the complete absence of

these, conversation would soon grind to a halt. Nonverbal cues also regulate the conversational flow, so that each person speaks in turn and there are few interruptions or long, uncomfortable silences. The management of turn-taking is a complex and subtle matter. In ordinary conversation people don't do it with words—they don't say "over to you" or "roger and out" when they're through talking. Yet most of the time the listener is ready to take up his end of the conversation, as if on cue. Sometimes he has already averted his eyes, changed his head position, and in other small ways anticipated the fact that his turn is coming. How can he tell that the other is about to give up the floor?

Some years ago a study done by Adam Kendon (as described in Chapter Nine) suggested that eye behavior is part of this cuing system. In a two-person conversation, the speaker glances at his companion from time to time and then looks away again, and his away glances last roughly as long as his contact glances do. As he comes to the end of his statement, though, he gives his listener a longer look and this apparently alerts the other so that he's ready to take his turn.

A more recent study suggests that there are a number of other turn-taking cues as well. Starkey Duncan, Jr., a University of Chicago professor, worked with two video-taped conversations: one between a therapist and a prospective patient, the other between the same therapist and a colleague. In each case, Duncan did an exhaustive analysis of the first nineteen minutes of the tape. It took him the better part of two academic years just to transcribe the verbal and nonverbal behavior, but when he was through he had discovered turn-taking cues in body motions, in what was said, and in the way it was said.

Looking at what was said, he found that each speaker used particular, stereotyped phrases that signaled that he (or she) was ready to give up the floor. They were awkward, uninformative—"but, uh," "or something," "you know"—and often uttered in a voice that trailed off across the phrase. Of course, there were grammatical clues, too, such as asking the listener a question. Duncan learned that in general, as a speaker winds up his statement, the pitch of his voice either rises (as in a question) or falls. A slight rasp, a bit of a drawl, a drop in volume, properly placed, all have turn-taking significance.

In body motion the clues were partly in gestures that stopped or relaxed. If the individual had been gesticulating, his hands become still. If his fist had been clenched or his ankle flexed, then fist or ankle noticeably relaxed. And he aimed his head at the listener, and held it that way. Duncan didn't record eye behavior because it was too difficult to judge from the video tapes; however, he believes that, in his study, gaze direction was probably synonymous with head direction. In any case, we probably learn at an early age that when we point our heads at another person, he reacts as if we were looking at him.

In general, it took a cluster of three floor-yielding cues occurring simultaneously or in tight sequence to get the message across, and even then there was simultaneous talking some of the time. Duncan believes that the turn-taking system, like most others, is vulnerable to outside interference. If the general noise level is high, if the topic is a sensitive one, if an individual becomes rather emotional and starts missing his cues, the system will be disrupted.

It stands to reason that the turn-taking system must also include floor-retaining signals—ways of hanging on to the speaker's role. Duncan turned up one such cue which seemed to occur at times when the speaker was almost, but not quite, ready to yield the floor: he would begin a sequence of yielding cues but as he did so his hands would be busy with gesticulations. He would keep on gesturing until he came to the end of what he had to say.

Sometimes a listener sees his turn coming up and prefers not to take it, so he communicates in what Duncan calls the "back channel." By nodding, murmuring encouragement, or even by chiming in and completing the speaker's sentence in unison with him, the listener can signal: Keep on talking. If he makes a short request for clarification, or briefly restates what the speaker has just finished saying, the message is the same.

The flexibility of this turn-taking system is impressive. There are so many interchangeable cues that turn-taking and floor-holding can be managed even over the telephone, where body signals can't be used, and only verbal and vocal clues are available. And as Erving Goffman has pointed out, Duncan's work indicates that an awesome amount of competency is required just to be able to pass the time of day with a friend. To say, then, that a child of the ghetto is "undersocialized" is inaccurate. He may be illiterate and he may not have acquired the skills necessary to get ahead in a competitive society, but if he can manage normal conversation he's very socialized indeed. Goffman concludes that when it comes to face-to-face encounters, the differences between "the crude and the cultivated" are slight in comparison to the similarities.

21 | The Future

Communication research has been around for more than twenty years, yet only in the last eight or nine have scientists and the general public, especially the young, become fascinated with the subject of nonverbal communication. And so one wonders: Why now?

I think one answer may be that there is today a general distrust of words, especially among the young. Life is so much more complex than it once was; parents and teachers are no longer the only or even the primary authority figures and children are bombarded with different opinions: by television, by radio, by films, and by what they read. When my daughter was four, she used to say with lofty skepticism, "You can't believe anything they say on the TV commercials." Older children hear politicians pay lip service to peace, equality, and the good life, and then on the newscasts they *see* poverty, anger, bigotry, war—life at its ugliest.

And so there's a distrust of words, together with a general feeling of alienation and a new groping for the comfort of personal relationships. We have also become much more visually oriented, more open to the idea of visible—body—communication. In the 1967 introduction to *Male and Female,* Margaret Mead wrote:

> The young are expressing themselves bodily, in forms designed to be viewed on TV rather than read about in magazines. Demonstrations characterized by strange and conspicuous body positions—sit-in, lie-in, sleep-in, bleed-in, be-in, love-in (in ice-cold ponds on the edge of spring)—have replaced the poster and the handout. Clothes and hairdo's have become vitally important indications of ethical and political attitudes. We have moved to a more visual period, where what is seen is more important than what is read, and what is experienced directly is valued over what is learned secondhand.

Encounter groups, too, with their emphasis on doing rather than saying—on touching, sniffing, staring, wrestling, acting out "nonverbal communication" in *their* special sense of the phrase—have contributed to the general *Zeitgeist*, the feeling of the times.

Although human communication is still virtually an infant science, it has already generated its share of ambitious prophecies and dire predictions. The prophets of gloom, for example, worry about the power of the would-be demagogue trained in nonverbal skills—about what a politician could do if he could project literally any image, any emotion, he wanted to, especially in this age of the televised political campaign.

Will people use the new knowledge about communication to manipulate others? Almost inevitably—but people have always manipulated other people. There have always been demagogues and individuals—as Paul Ekman's studies show—who could lie convincingly.

They may now become even more persuasive, more skilled at projecting a false image, but as the public also becomes more aware of nonverbal signals, the con man's gains should be small and short lived.

Though the average person may learn to tell lies more skillfully, I doubt whether it will be possible to make him letter-perfect, at least in face-to-face situations. There are too many nonverbal signals that operate on a subliminal level—from palming to moving in synchrony to micromomentary facial expressions—and for the most part the subliminal signals probably can't be consciously controlled. There are some people who can deliberately coordinate the behavior of face, hands, eyes, body, while still keeping up an intelligible conversation, but one wonders whether their special skill is not, perhaps, the ability to lie to and momentarily convince themselves, rather than any ability to consciously control their body language.

In direct contrast to those who worry about lessons in lying, there is a tendency among some laymen to see "communication" as a cure-all: if people could just learn to really communicate with each other, they say, the generation gap would disappear, racial tensions would dissipate, and everybody would be much freer and happier. Unfortunately, human motivations and relationships are generally pretty tangled and cures aren't that simple. It's certainly true that men of good will probably will be intrigued and reassured to learn that there are cultural differences in the body code and that this accounts for some of the strangeness they sense when in the presence of someone from another race or culture; but the true bigot is unlikely to be influenced. Bigotry has its roots in deep, seldom-expressed fears and desires— the need, for example, to have someone to look down on, a focus for one's hatreds and fears and one's need to feel superior. Having some of the strangeness in the physical presence of the other explained away will make little impression on this kind of individual.

But it would be as unintelligent to underrate as to overrate the potential of human-communication studies. In some ways, they are already beginning to change the way we think, and they will continue to do so. Language specialists may soon be taught the kinesics of a foreign language along with its grammar and vocabulary, for attempts are already being made to teach the emblems— the specific gestural vocabulary—of particular languages and cultures.

Architects and city planners are becoming more aware of men's reactions to the space around them, and may design more comfortable buildings, more livable cities. Investigations of what Edward Hall calls microspace have already led to a whole new field of study— environmental psychology. Within the limits of what we're willing to spend—for research and to implement its findings—this could be an influential new science.

As it becomes possible to compare the new behavior of men with that of the other primates, we may learn more about evolution and about the very nature of man. And certainly, from films and film analysis, we should be able to learn more about child development and about relationships within the family.

But what does the new nonverbal research mean to the individual?

During the two years I've been intensively exposed to it, I've found that bits of body language can sometimes be translated into a ploy. I remember, for example, riding alone one day in an elevator with a distinguished-looking elderly man whom I knew by sight. Though he had never said a word to me before, on this particular occasion he began a conversation. I realized later that it was actually I who had made the first move in the encounter. When I got into the elevator, instead of standing with eyes front, facing the door, I tucked myself back into a corner so that I stood with my body pointed toward the man. Although I didn't actually look at him, that, apparently, was enough. Since then, I've used body orientation sometimes in similar circumstances as the opening gambit in a conversation. It works more often than not. But I am still, I think, like the beginner who knows exactly twelve words of a language: I try them out now and then, hopefully, hesitantly, but I don't really expect to get across anything complicated and I'm always surprised and delighted when people understand me at all. I know I'm a long way from the point where I'll be able—as Ray Birdwhistell puts it—to "communicate on purpose."

What I've really learned to do best is to decipher my own behavior. Halfway through a conversation, I'll realize that I'm sharing postures comfortably with a friend, or that I've just run one hand over my hair in a perfect S-groom, palming all the way; or it will come to me that I've been avoiding somebody's eyes, or that I'm leaning back, barricarded behind my own folded arms. I've caught myself echoing phrases and gestures, picking up rhythms, and literally backing into corners for various reasons.

I pick up clues from other people's behavior, too, but am cautious about interpreting them. Human communication is so incredibly complex that it has no hard-and-fast rules, and in the absence of such rules I know that I, like everyone else, have a tendency to see only what I want to see and to attend only to what it's convenient to know. On the other hand, these days when I have a sudden attack of intuition—a really strong feeling that I *know* how somebody is reacting, or what they're really getting at—I tend to trust my intuition, especially if I can pin down some of the body signals it's based on.

Perhaps the best thing to say about nonverbal communication from the *layman's* point of view is that learning about it is great fun. People are enormously and beautifully sensitive to one another—and they don't even know it. When they begin to move together, when they are caught up together in the current of words and body motions, they become like an incredibly integrated, fine-tuned, responsive system. As we learn more about this, as our sensitivities increase, there should be a new kind of sharing, a special awareness, and new pleasures that we can only guess at now.

Bibliography

Chapter 1: The Fledgling Science
Efron, David, *Gesture and Environment,* The Hague: Mouton, 1941, 1972. Originally published in 1941.
Sapir, Edward, in *Selected Writings of Edward Sapir,* D. G. Mandelbaum ed., Berkeley and Los Angeles: University of California Press, 1949, pp. 533–543.

Chapter 2: Gender Signals
Based partly on interviews with Ray L. Birdwhistell.
Of general interest—very relevant, very readable, or both:
Birdwhistell, Ray L., *Kinesics and Context,* Philadelphia: University of Pennsylvania Press, 1970.
Mead, Margaret, *Sex and Temperament in Three Primitive Societies,* New York: Dell, 1935, 1950, 1963.

Chapter 3: Courting Behaviors
Based partly on interviews with Albert E. Scheflen, Ray L. Birdwhistell, and Adam Kendon.
Of general interest:
Scheflen, Albert E., "Quasi-Courtship Behavior in Psychotherapy," *Psychiatry,* vol. 28, no. 3, pp. 245–257, 1965.

Chapter 4: The Silent, Celluloid World of Kinesics
Based partly on interviews with Ray L. Birdwhistell and Albert E. Scheflen.
Of general interest:
Birdwhistell, Ray L., *Kinesics and Context*, op. cit.

Research references:

Birdwhistell, Ray L., *Introduction to Kinesics,* (Photo-offset) Foreign Service Institute, Louisville: University of Louisville Press, 1952. Now available in microfilm only, from University Microfilms, Inc., 313 North First St., Ann Arbor, Mich.

Scheflen, Albert E., "Communication and Regulation in Psychotherapy," *Psychiatry,* vol. 26, no. 2, pp. 126–136, 1963.

Chapter 5: The Body is the Message

Based on interviews with Ray L. Birdwhistell.

Chapter 6: Greetings from a Very Old Primate

Based partly on interviews with Adam Kendon.

Research references:

Kendon, A., and A. Ferber, "Studies in Human Greetings," research in progress.

Eibl-Eibesfeldt, Irenäus, *Ethology. The Biology of Behavior,* New York: Holt, 1970.

Freedman, Daniel G., "A Biological View of Man's Social Behavior," in William Etkin, *Social Behavior from Fish To Man,* Chicago: The University of Chicago Press, 1967.

Goodall, Jane van Lawick, "In the Gombe Stream Chimpanzees," in *Primates: Studies in Adaptation and Variability,* Phyllis Jay ed., New York: Holt, 1968.

La Barre, Weston, "The Cultural Basis of Emotions and Gestures," *Journal of Personality,* vol. 16, no. 1, pp. 49–68, 1947.

Chapter 7: The Human Face

Based partly on an interview with Paul Ekman.

Of general interest:

Ekman, Paul, Wallace V. Friesen, and Phoebe Ellsworth, *Emotion in the Human Face,* New York; Pergamon, 1971.

Research references:

Andrew, Richard J., "The Origins of Facial Expressions," *Scientific American,* vol. 213, pp. 88–94, 1965.

Argyle, Michael, *Social Interaction,* London: Methuen, 1969.

Darwin, Charles, *The Expression of the Emotions in Man and Animals,* London: Murray, 1872.

226 *Inside Intuition*

Davey, A. G., "How Subliminal Is Your Persuasion," *New Society,* May 21, pp. 871–872, 1970.

Eibl-Eibesfeldt, Irenäus, *Ethology,* op. cit.

Ekman, Paul, and Wallace V. Friesen, "Nonverbal Behavior in Psychotherapy Research," in *Research in Psychotherapy,* vol. 3, J. Shlien ed., American Psychological Association, 1968, pp. 179–216.

———, "The Repertoire of Nonverbal Behavior: Categories, Origins, Usage, and Coding," *Semiotica,* vol. 1, no. 1, pp. 49–98, 1969.

———, "Nonverbal Leakage and Clues to Deception," *Psychiatry,* vol. 32, no. 1, pp. 88–106, 1969.

Ekman, Paul, E. Richard Sorenson, and Wallace V. Friesen, "Pan-Cultural Elements in Facial Displays of Emotion," *Science,* vol. 164, pp. 86–88, 1969.

Ekman, Paul, Wallace V. Friesen, and Silvan S. Tomkins, "Facial Affect Scoring Technique: A First Validity Study," *Semiotica,* vol. 3, pp. 37–58, 1971.

Freud, Sigmund, "Fragment of an Analysis of a Case of Hysteria (1905)," *Collected Papers,* vol. 3, New York: Basic Books, 1959.

Fulcher, J. S., "'Voluntary' Facial Expression in Blind and Seeing Children," *Archives of Psychology,* no. 272, 38, pp. 1–49, 1942.

Goodenough, F. L., "Expressions of the Emotions in a Blind-Deaf Child," *Journal of Abnormal and Social Psychology,* vol. 27, pp. 328–333, 1932.

Haggard, Ernest A., and Kenneth S. Isaacs, "Micromentary Facial Expressions as Indicators of Ego Mechanisms in Psychotherapy," in *Methods of Research in Psychotherapy,* Louis A. Gottschalk and Arthur H. Auerbach eds., New York: Appleton-Century-Crofts, 1966.

Izard, C. E., "The Emotions and Emotion Concepts in Personality Culture Research," in *Handbook of Modern Personality Theory,* R. B. Cattell, ed., Chicago: Aldine, 1970.

———, *The Face of Emotion,* New York: Appleton-Century-Crofts, 1971.

La Barre, Weston, "The Cultural Basis of Emotions and Gestures," op. cit.

Landis, C. "The Interpretation of Facial Expression in Emotion," *Journal of General Psychology,* vol. 2, pp. 59–72, 1929.

Orwell, George, *1984.* New York: Harcourt Brace, 1949.

Thompson, J., "Development of Facial Expressions of Emotion in Blind and Seeing Children," *Archives of Psychology*, no. 264, 37, pp. 1–47, 1940.

Tomkins, Silvan S., *Affect, Imagery, Consciousness, Vol 1. The Positive Affects*, New York: Springer, 1962.

Chapter 8: What the Eyes Tell

Based partly on an interview with Ralph Exline.

Of general interest:

Exline, Ralph, and Lewis C. Winters, "Affective Relations and Mutual Glances in Dyads," in *Affect, Cognition and Personality*, Silvan S. Tomkins and C. E. Izard, eds., New York: Springer, 1965, pp. 319–350.

——, and Absalom M. Yellin, "Eye Contact as a Sign between Man and Monkey," unpublished paper, University of Delaware.

Hess, Eckhard H., "Attitude and Pupil Size," *Scientific American*, vol. 212, pp. 46–54, 1965.

Kendon, Adam, "Some Functions of Gaze-Direction in Social Interaction," *Acta Psychologica*, vol. 26, pp. 22–63, 1967.

Tomkins, Silvan S. *Affect, Imagery, Consciousness, Vol. II. The Negative Affects*, New York: Springer, 1963.

Research references:

Argyle, Michael, *Social Interaction*, op. cit.

Exline, Ralph V., "Explorations in the Process of Person Perception: Visual Interaction in Relation to Competition, Sex, and Need for Affiliation," *Journal of Personality*, vol. 31, no. 1, pp. 1–20, 1963.

——, David Gray, and Dorothy Schuette, "Visual Behavior in a Dyad as Affected by Interview Content and Sex of Respondent," *Journal of Personality and Social Psychology*, vol. 1, no. 3, pp. 201–209, 1965.

——, and L. C. Winters, "The Effects of Cognitive Difficulty and Cognitive Style upon Eye to Eye Contact in Interviews," paper presented at the meeting of the Eastern Psychological Association, Atlantic City, 1965.

——, John Thibaut, Carole Brannan, and Peter Gumpert, "Visual Interaction in Relation to Machiavellianism and an Unethical Act," in *Studies in Machiavellianism*, R. Christie and Florence Geis, eds., London: Academic, 1966.

——, and David Messick, "The Effects of Dependency and Social

Reinforcement upon Visual Behaviour During an Interview," *British Journal of Social and Clinical Psychology*, vol. 6, pp. 256–266, 1967.

Goffman, Erving, *Behavior in Public Places*, New York: Free Press, 1963.

Hall, Edward T. *The Hidden Dimension*, New York: Doubleday, 1966.

Hess, Eckhard H., "Pupillometric Assessment," in *Research in Psychotherapy*, vol. 3, J. Shlien, ed., American Psychological Association, 1968, pp. 573–583.

Hess, Eckhard H., Allan L. Seltzer, and John M. Shlien, "Pupil Response of Hetero- and Homosexual Males to Pictures of Men and Woman: A Pilot Study," *Journal of Abnormal Psychology*, vol. 70, no. 3, pp. 165–168, 1965.

La Barre, Weston, comment on "Proxemics," by Edward T. Hall, *Current Anthropology*, vol. 9, no. 2–3, pp. 101–102, 1968.

Nielsen, G., *Studies in Self-Confrontation,* Copenhagen: Munksgaard, 1964.

Russo, Nancy J., "Eye Contact, Inter-Personal Distance and Equilibrium Theory," unpublished doctoral dissertation, Cornell University, Ithaca, New York, 1970.

Schaller, George B., *The Year of the Gorilla*, Chicago: University of Chicago Press, 1964.

Sartre, Jean-Paul, *Being and Nothingness*, Hazel E. Barnes trans., New York: Philosophical Library, 1956. Originally published in Paris in 1942.

Vine, Ian, "Communication by Facial-Visual Signals," in *Social Behaviour in Animals and Man,* J. H. Crook ed., London: Academic, 1970.

Weisbrod, Rita, "Looking Behavior in a Discussion Group." Term paper submitted for Psychology 546 under the direction of Professor Longabaugh, Cornell University, Ithaca, New York, 1965.

Chapter 9: The Dance of the Hands

Based partly on interviews with Paul Ekman, Adam Kendon, and Albert Scheflen.

Of general interest:

Ekman, Paul, and Wallace V. Friesen "The Repertoire of Nonverbal Behavior: Categories, Origins, Usage, and Coding," op. cit.

Research references:

Argyle, Michael, *Social Interaction*, op. cit.

Dittmann, Alan, "The Relationship between Body Movements and Moods in Interviews," *Journal of Consulting Psychology*, vol. 26, pp. 480, 1962.

Efron, David, *Gesture and Environment*, op. cit.

Kendon, Adam, "Some Relationships between Body Motion and Speech: An Analysis of an Example," in *Studies in Dyadic Interaction: A Research Conference*, A. Seigman and B. Pope eds., New York: Pergamon, 1970.

La Barre, Weston, "Paralinguistics, Kinesics and Cultural Anthropology," in *Approaches to Semiotics*, Thomas A. Sebeok, Alfred S. Hayes, and Mary Catherine Bateson eds., The Hague: Mouton, 1964, pp. 191–220.

Mead, Margaret, *Male and Female, A Study of the Sexes in a Changing World*, New York: Dell, 1949.

Murphy, Gardner, Book Review in *The Annals of the American Academy*, vol. 220, pp. 268–269, 1942.

Rosenfeld, Howard M., "Instrumental Affiliative Functions of Facial and Gestural Expressions," *Journal of Personality and Social Psychology*, vol. 4, no. 1, pp. 65–72, 1966.

Ruesch, Jurgen, and Weldon Kees, *Non-Verbal Communication*, Berkeley: University of California Press, 1956.

Saitz, Robert, and Edward Cervenka, *Handbook of Gestures: Colombia and the United States*, The Hague: Mcuton.

Chapter 10: The Messages in Distance and Location

Based partly on an interview with Edward Hall.

Of general interest:

Hall, Edward T., *The Silent Language*, New York: Fawcett, 1959.

———, *The Hidden Dimension*, New York: Doubleday, 1966.

Sommer, Robert, *Personal Space. The Behavioral Basis of Design*, Englewood Cliffs, New Jersey: Prentice-Hall, 1969.

Kendon, Adam, "The Role of Visible Behaviour in the Organization of Social Interaction," in *Expressive Movement and Nonverbal Behaviour*, Mario von Cranach and Ian Vine eds., London: Academic.

Research references:

Argyle, Michael, *Social Interaction*, op. cit.

Calhoun, John B., "Population Density and Social Pathology," *Scientific American*, vol. 206, pp. 139–146, 1962.

Freedman, Jonathan L., "The Crowd: Maybe Not So Madding after All," *Psychology Today,* September, pp. 58–61, 1971.

Hall, Edward T., "Proxemics," *Current Anthropology,* vol. 9, no. 2–3, pp. 83–108, 1968.

———, "Psychological Aspects of Foreign Policy," hearings before the Committee on Foreign Relations, United States Senate, June 5, 19, and 20, 1969, U.S. Government Printing Office, Washington, D.C.

Kinzel, Augustus F., "Body-Buffer Zone in Violent Prisoners," *American Journal of Psychiatry,* vol. 127, no. 1, 1970.

Kleck, Robert, et al., "Effect of Stigmatizing Conditions on the Use of Personal Space," *Psychological Reports,* vol. 23, pp. 111–118, 1968.

Little, Kenneth B., "Personal Space," *Journal of Experimental Social Psychology,* vol. 1, pp. 237–247, 1965.

Mehrabian, A., "The Inference of Attitudes from the Posture, Orientation, and Distance of a Communication," *Journal of Consulting Psychology,* vol. 32, pp. 296–308, 1968.

Norum, Gary, Nancy Jo Russo, and Robert Sommer, "Seating Patterns and Group Task," *Psychology in the Schools,* vol. IV, no. 3, pp. 276–280, 1967.

Sommer, Robert, "Leadership and Group Geography," *Sociometry,* vol. 24, pp. 99–109, 1961.

———, "The Ecology of Privacy," *The Library Quarterly,* vol. 36, no. 3, July, 1966.

Sommer, Robert, and Franklin D. Becker, "Territorial Defense and the Good Neighbor," *Journal of Personality and Social Psychology,* vol. 11, no. 2, pp. 85–92, 1969.

Strodtbeck, Fred L., and L. Harmon Hook, "The Social Dimensions of a Twelve-Man Jury Table," *Sociometry,* vol. 24, pp. 397–415, 1961.

Chapter 11: Interpreting Postures

Of general interest:

Scheflen, Albert E., "The Significance of Posture in Communication Systems," *Psychiatry,* vol. 27, no. 4, pp. 316–331, 1964.

Research references:

Argyle, Michael, *Social Interaction,* op. cit.

Charney, E. Joseph, "Psychosomatic manifestations of rapport in psychotherapy," *Psychosomatic Medicine*, vol. 28, pp. 305-315, 1966.

Deutsch, Felix, "Analysis of Postural Behavior," *Psychoanalytic Quarterly*, vol. 16, pp. 195–213, 1947.

Foulkes, David, *The Psychology of Sleep*. New York: Scribner, 1966.

Goffman, Erving. *Asylums*. Garden City, New York: Anchor Books, 1961.

Hewes, Gordon W., "The Anthropology of Posture," *Scientific American*, vol. 196, pp. 122–132, 1957.

Kendon, Adam, "The Role of Visible Behaviour in the Organization of Social Interaction," op. cit.

Lowen, Alexander, *The Betrayal of the Body*, London: Collier Books, 1967.

Macdonald, Dwight, Introduction in *The Tales of Hoffman*, Mark L. Levine, George C. McNamee and Daniel Greenberg, eds. New York: Bantam, 1970.

Machotka, P., "Body Movement as Communication," in *Dialogue*: *Behavioral Science Research*. Western Interstate Commission for Higher Education, Boulder, Colorado, 1965.

Mehrabian, Albert, "Relationship of Attitude to Seated Posture, Orientation and Distance," *Journal of Personality and Social Psychology*, vol. 10, no. 1, pp. 26–30, 1968.

——, "Communication without words," *Psychology Today*, September, 1968,

——, "Significance of Posture and Position in the Communication of Attitude and Status Relationships," *Psychological Bulletin*, Vol. 71, pp. 359–372, 1969.

Scheflen, Albert E., *The Stream and Structure of Communicational Behavior*, Bloomington and London: Indiana University Press, in press.

Schutz, William C., *Joy*, New York: Grove Press, 1967.

Chapter 12: Body Rhythms

Based partly on interviews with William Condon and Paul Byers.
Of general interest:
Condon, W. S., "Linguistic-Kinesic Research and Dance Therapy" in *Proceedings* of the third annual conference of the American Dance Therapy Association, 1968.
Research references:
Byers, Paul and Happie Byers, "Nonverbal Communication and the Education of Children," in *Functions of Communication* (tenta-

tive title), Courtney Cazdan, Vera John and Dell Hymes, eds., To be published by Teachers College Press.

Condon, W. S. and W. D. Ogston, "Sound Film Analysis of Normal and Pathological Behavior Patterns," *The Journal of Nervous and Mental Disease*, vol. 143, no. 4, pp. 338–347, 1966.

———, "A Segmentation of Behavior," *Journal of Psychiatric Research*, vol. 5, pp. 221–235, 1967.

Condon, William S., William D. Ogston, and Larry V. Pacoe, "Three Faces of Eve Revisited: A Study of Transient Microstrabismus," *Journal of Abnormal Psychology*, vol. 74, no. 5, pp. 618–620, 1969.

Eibl-Eibesfeldt, Irenäus, *Ethology*, op. cit.

Kendon, Adam, "Movement Coordination in Social Interaction: Some Examples Described," *Acta Psychologica*, vol. 32, pp. 1–25, 1970.

Chapter *13*: The Rhythms of the Human Encounter

Based partly on interviews with Eliot Chapple.

Of general interest:

Chapple, Eliot D., *Culture and Biological Man*, New York: Holt, 1970.

Chapple, Eliot D., and L. R. Sayles, *The Measure of Management*, New York: Macmillan, 1961.

Research references:

Chapple, Eliot D., "The Standard Experimental (Stress) Interview as Used in Interaction Chronograph Investigation," *Human Organization*, vol. 12, no. 2, pp. 23–32, 1953.

———, "Toward a Mathematical Model of Interaction: Some Preliminary Considerations," in *Explorations in Mathematical Anthropology*, Paul Kay ed., Cambridge, Mass.: M.I.T., 1970.

———, et al., "Measurement of the Activity Patterns of Schizophrenic Patients," *Journal of Nervous and Mental Disease*, vol. 137, pp. 258–267, 1963.

———, et al., "Principles of Programmed Interaction Therapy," in preparation.

Goldman-Eisler, Frieda, "On the Variability of the Speed of Talking and on Its Relations to the Length of Utterances in Conversation," *British Journal of Psychology*, vol. 45, pp. 94–107, 1954.

Hayes, Donald P., Leo Meltzer, and Gary D. Bouma, "Activity as a Determinant of Interpersonal Perception," American Psychological Association *Proceedings*, 76th convention, pp. 417–418, 1968.

Matarazzo, Joseph, "A Technique for Studying Changes in Interview Behavior," in *Research in Psychotherapy*, Washington, D.C.: American Psychological Association, 1957.

Chapter 14: Communicating by Smell

Of general interest:

Wiener, Harry, "External Chemical Messengers: I. Emission and Reception in Man," *New York State Journal of Medicine*, vol. 66, no. 24, pp. 3153–3170, 1966.

Research references:

Comfort, Alex, "Human Aromas: the Language of Smell," *Intellectual Digest*, May–June, pp. 87–93, 1971.

Eibl-Eibesfeldt, Irenäus, *Ethology*, op. cit.

Hall, Edward T. *The Hidden Dimension,* New York: Doubleday, 1966.

Rosebury, Theodor, *Life on Man*, New York: Viking, 1969.

Smith, K., G. F. Thompson, and H . D. Koster, "Sweat in Schizophrenic Patients: Identification of the Odorous Substance," *Science*, vol. 166, pp. 398–399, 1969.

Wiener, Harry, "External Chemical Messengers: II. Natural History of Schizophrenia," *New York State Journal of Medicine*, vol. 67, no. 9, pp. 1144–1165, 1967.

———, "External Chemical Messengers: III. Mind and Body in Schizophrenia," *New York State Journal of Medicine*, vol. 67, no. 10, pp. 1287–1310, 1967.

Chapter 15: Communicating by Touch

Of general interest:

Frank, Lawrence K., "Tactile Communication," *Genetic Psychology Monographs*, vol. 56, pp. 209–225, 1957. Reprinted in *The Rhetoric of Nonverbal Communication*, Haig A. Bosmajian ed., Glenview, Illinois: Scott, Foresman, 1971, pp. 34–55.

Montagu, Ashley, *Touching. The Human Significance of the Skin*, New York: Columbia, 1971.

Research references:

Goffman, Erving, *Relations in Public.* New York: Basic Books, 1971.

Hall, Edward T., *The Hidden Dimension,* op. cit.

Jourard, Sidney, "Out of Touch! The Body Taboo," *New Society*, November, 1967.

———, *Disclosing Man to Himself,* Princeton, N.J.: Van Nostrand, 1968.

Mead, Margaret, *Male and Female,* op. cit.

Chapter *16*: The Lessons of the Womb

Of general interest

Liley, Dr. H. M. I., with Beth Day, *Modern Motherhood,* New York: Random House, 1966.

Montagu, Ashley, *Touching: The Human Significance of the Skin,* New York: Columbia, 1971.

Truby, Henry, "Prenatal, Neonatal, and Alphabetistic Aspects of Language Acquisition," paper presented at meeting of the International Linguistic Association, New York, 1970.

Research references:

Eibl-Eibesfeldt, Irenäus, *Ethology,* op. cit.

Fraiberg, Selma, *The Magic Years,* New York: Scribner, 1959.

Martin, R. D., "The Biology of Human Behaviour," op. cit.

Meerloo, Joost, "Rhythm in Babies and Adults," from *Unobtrusive Communication,* Assen, the Netherlands: Royal Van Gorcum Ltd., 1964. Reprinted in *The Rhetoric of Nonverbal Communication,* Haig A. Bosmajian ed., Glenview, Illinois: Scott, Foresman, pp. 57–67, 1971.

Morris, Desmond, *The Naked Ape,* New York: Dell, 1967.

Robson, K. S., "The Role of Eye-to-eye Contact in Maternal-Infant Attachment," *Journal of Child Psychology,* vol. 8, pp. 13–25, 1967.

Tomkins, Silvan S., *Affect, Imagery, Consciousness,* op. cit.

Vine, Ian, "Communication by Facial-Visual Signals," op. cit.

Chapter *17*: The Nonverbal Code of Childhood

Of general interest:

Brannigan, Christopher, and Dr. David Humphries, "I See What You Mean . . . ," *New Scientist,* May 22, 1969, pp. 406–408.

Grant, Ewan, "Face to Face," *New Society,* May 7, 1970, pp. 769–771.

Research references:

Blurton Jones, N. G., "An Ethological Study of Some Aspects of Social Behaviour of Children in Nursery School," in *Primate Ethology,* Desmond Morris ed., Garden City, New York: Anchor Books, 1967, pp. 437–463.

Currie, K. H., and C. R. Brannigan, "Behavioural Analysis and

Modification with an Autistic Child," in *Behaviour Studies in Psychiatry*, C. and S. J. Hutt eds., London: Pergamon, 1970.

Chapter 18: Clues to Character
Based partly on interviews with Martha Davis and Irmgard Bartenieff.
Of general interest:
Lamb, Warren, and David Turner, *Management Behaviour*, New York; International Universities Press, 1969.
Lomax Alan, *Folk Song, Style and Culture*, Washington, D.C.: American Association for the Advancement of Science, 1968.
Research references:
Bartenieff, Irmgard, and Martha Ann Davis, "Effort-Shape Analysis of Movement. The Unity of Expression and Function," 1965. Available from the Dance Notation Bureau, 8 East 12th Street, New York, N.Y. 10003.
———, "An Analysis of the Movement Behavior within a Group Psychotherapy Session." Presented at the conference of the American Group Psychotherapy Association, January, 1968.
Davis, Martha Ann, "An Effort-Shape Analysis of a Family Therapy Session," 1966. Available from the Dance Notation Bureau, 8 East 12th Street, New York, N.Y. 10003.
———, "Movement Characteristics of Hospitalized Psychiatric Patients" in *Proceedings* of the American Dance Therapy Association Conference, October, 1970.
Dell, Cecily, *A Primer for Movement Description*, New York: Dance Notation Bureau, 1970.
Dittmann, Allen T., Morris B. Parloff, and Donald S. Boomer, "Facial and Bodily Expression: A Study of Receptivity of Emotional Cues," *Psychiatry*, vol. 28, no. 3, pp. 239–244, 1965.
Kestenberg, Dr. Judith, "The Role of Movement Patterns in Development." Published originally in *Psychoanalytic Quarterly*. Available from the Dance Notation Bureau, 8 East 12th Street, New York, N.Y. 10003.

Chapter 19: Public Order
Based partly on interviews with Erving Goffman.
Of general interest:
Goffman, Erving, *Relations in Public*, New York: Basic Books, 1971.

Research references:
Goffman, Erving, *The Presentation of Self in Everyday Life,* Garden City, New York: Anchor Books, 1959.
——, *Asylums,* op. cit.
——, *Behavior in Public Places,* op. cit.
——, *Interaction Ritual,* Garden City, New York: Anchor Books, 1967.
Macdonald, Dwight, Introduction in *The Tales of Hoffman,* op. cit.

Chapter 20: Making Conversation

Research references:
Argyle, Michael, *Social Interaction,* op. cit.
Duncan, Starkey, Jr., "Some Signals and Rules for Taking Speaking Turns in Conversations," unpublished, 1971.
Goffman, Erving, *Relations in Public,* op. cit.
Kendon, Adam, "Some Functions of Gaze-Direction in Social Interaction," op. cit.

Chapter 21: The Future

Research references:
Mead, Margaret, *Male and Female,* op. cit.

Index